Lake District

Text: Terry Marsh
Photography: Terry Marsh, Bill Birkett, John Curtis, Audrey Marsh, Charles Nicholas
Editorial: Ark Creative (UK) Ltd
Design: Ark Creative (UK) Ltd

This product includes mapping data licensed from Ordnance Survey® with the permission of the Controller of Her Majesty's Stationery Office.
© Crown Copyright 2009. All rights reserved. Licence number 150002047. Ordnance Survey, the OS symbol and Pathfinder are registered trademarks and Explorer, Landranger and Outdoor Leisure are trademarks of the Ordnance Survey, the national mapping agency of Great Britain.

ISBN: 978-1-85458-523-3

If you find an inaccuracy in either the text or maps, please write to Crimson Publishing at the address below.

First published 2001
Revised and reprinted 2004, 2005, 2008, 2009.

This edition first published in Great Britain 2009 by Crimson Publishing, a division of:
Crimson Business Ltd
Westminster House, Kew Road
Richmond, Surrey, TW9 2ND

www.totalwalking.co.uk

Printed in Singapore. 7/09

Front cover: Brothers Water, looking towards Place Fell
Previous page: Greendale, near Wastwater

Contents

Keymap

SCALE 1:250 000 or 1 INCH to 4 MILES *1CM to 2.5KM*

KEYMAP HEIGHTS SHOWN IN METRES

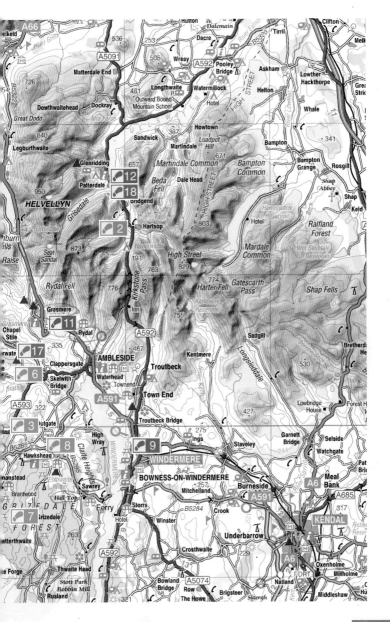

At-a-glance

1

Newlands Valley

2

Brothers Water

3

Tarn Hows by Tom Gill

4

Barrow

• **Gold mine** • **quiet valley** • **ancient church** • **ancient school**	• **Lakeside** • **woodland birds** • **ancient hall** • **waterside path**	• **Waterfalls** • **glorious scenery** • **upland tarn** • **woodland wildlife**	• **Mountain vista** • **heathland views** • **pretty village** • **good pubs**

Walk Distance
1½ miles (2.4km)
Time
1 hour
Refreshments
Teas, Low Snab Farm; pubs in Braithwaite; family facilities in Keswick

Walk Distance
2½ miles (4km)
Time
1½ hours
Refreshments
Brothers Water Inn, and in Patterdale

Walk Distance
1½ miles (2.4km)
Time
1 hour
Refreshments
Coniston

Walk Distance
3½ miles (5.6km)
Time
2 hours
Refreshments
Braithwaite has a couple of family friendly pubs; family facilities in Keswick

Fell and farm tracks; one stream crossing; some boggy ground

Woodland tracks, *slippery when wet;* lakeside path with tree roots to cross

Woodland paths; tarnside track

Steadily rising fell path; rocky ridge and long grassy descent

p. 18

p. 22

p. 26

p. 30

Walk Completed ☐

Walk Completed ☐

Walk Completed ☐

Walk Completed ☐

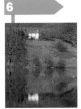

5

6

7

8

Whinlatter Forest

Loughrigg Tarn

Grizedale Forest

Latterbarrow

• Lovely views • woodland wildlife • forest trails • scent of pine	• White-water falls • walled tracks • lakeside views • riverside path	• Woodland trails • forest sculptures • waterfalls • mountain tarn	• Massive cairn • stunning views • flora and fauna • woodland trail

Walk Distance
1½ miles (2.4km)

Time
1 hour

Refreshments
Whinlatter Visitor Centre

Walk Distance
2¾ miles (4.5km)

Time
1½ hours

Refreshments
Pub at Skelwith Bridge and café in Kirkstone Galleries

Walk Distance
3 miles (4.8km)

Time
2 hours

Refreshments
Grizedale Tea Room

Walk Distance
3½ miles (5.6km)

Time
2 hours

Refreshments
Hawkshead has numerous family-friendly pubs and cafés

Steep forest paths and tracks

Narrow paths through bracken; rough tracks and lanes

Woodland tracks and stony paths

Good paths and tracks; muddy woodland trails; some stiles to cross

p.34

p. 38

p. 42

p. 46

Walk Completed ☐

Walk Completed ☐

Walk Completed ☐

Walk Completed ☐

9 ➤

10 ➤

11 ➤

12 ➤

Orrest Head and Allen Knot

Buttermere

Rydal Water

Silver Bay

• Iron Age hillfort	• Secret tunnel	• **Wordsworth home**	• Cave
• superb scenery	• woodland birds	• waterfall	• picnic areas
• outstanding view	• lakeside paths	• coffin stone	• old quarry
• interesting tree	• views	• lake & riverside	• juniper bushes

Walk Distance	**Walk Distance**	**Walk Distance**	**Walk Distance**
4½ miles (7.2km)	4½ miles (7.2km)	3½ miles (5.6km)	3½ miles (5.6km)
Time	**Time**	**Time**	**Time**
2 hours	2½ hours	2 hours	2 hours
Refreshments	**Refreshments**	**Refreshments**	**Refreshments**
Windermere has numerous pubs and cafés	Two pubs at Buttermere (both welcome children) and a café	Both Rydal and nearby Grasmere have family-friendly pubs	Patterdale pubs serve bar meals and welcome children

Woodland paths; farm tracks and fields	Good paths throughout; a little road walking	Riverside paths; fell tracks and fields; rocky shoulder	Bracken and juniper fell slopes to cross; rocky descent to Silver Bay

p. 51	**p. 56**	**p. 60**	**p. 64**
Walk Completed ☐	Walk Completed ☐	Walk Completed ☐	Walk Completed ☐

13

14

15

16

Rannerdale	*Castlerigg and Tewet Tarn*	*Cat Bells*	*Blawith Common and Beacon Tarn*
• Ridge walking • cascades • outstanding view • secluded valley	• Prehistoric site • upland tarn • ancient bridge • old church	• Ridge walking • old road • outstanding view • rocky scrambles	• Views of high fells • Cumbria Way • isolated tarn • ... and a mystery
Walk Distance 4½ miles (7.2km) **Time** 2½ hours **Refreshments** Buttermere has two pubs and a café	**Walk Distance** 4 miles (6.4km) **Time** 2 hours **Refreshments** Keswick has numerous family-friendly pubs and cafés	**Walk Distance** 3½ miles (5.6km) **Time** 2 hours **Refreshments** Portinscale and Keswick	**Walk Distance** 3½ miles (5.6km) **Time** 2½ hours **Refreshments** Pub in Torver, but otherwise Coniston has a host of family-friendly facilities
Good paths; fell ridge walking; steep, stony descent	Back lanes; farm fields; access tracks; stiles and hummocky fellsides	Steep ascent and descent; rocky outcrops	Some busy road walking to start; brackeny fells, muddy when wet, and minor unenclosed road to finish
p.68	**p. 72**	**p. 77**	**p. 81**
Walk Completed ☐	Walk Completed ☐	Walk Completed ☐	Walk Completed ☐

Longer walks of 5 miles or more

17	18	19	20

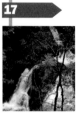
Elterwater

Grisedale

Latrigg

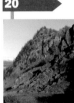
Castle Crag

• White-water falls • nice woodland • riverside walks • old bridge	• Mountain views • moraines • waterfalls • scenery	• Old bobbin mill • river scenery • outstanding view • old bridge	• Cave • riverside walks • woodland • wonderful view
Walk Distance 5½ miles (8.9km)	**Walk Distance** 6 miles (9.7km)	**Walk Distance** 5 miles (8km)	**Walk Distance** 5 miles (8km)
Time 3 hours	**Time** 3 hours	**Time** 3 hours	**Time** 3 hours
Refreshments Pubs at Elterwater and Skelwith Bridge, café at Kirkstone Galleries	**Refreshments** Patterdale pubs (family-friendly); shop	**Refreshments** Keswick town centre has numerous family-friendly pubs and cafés	**Refreshments** Seatoller (café)
Good paths all the way; spectacular waterfalls and riverside paths	Fell paths, farm tracks and rugged mountain terrain	Old railway trackbed; one steepish climb on country lane; grassy ridge and gradual descent	Stony tracks; rocky scrambling (optional); riverside paths; numerous tree roots and rocky sections; one brief, low rocky ledge to cross
p. 85	p. 90	p. 95	p. 100
Walk Completed ☐	Walk Completed ☐	Walk Completed ☐	Walk Completed ☐

Introduction

The routes and information in this book have been devised specifically with families and children in mind. All the walks include points of interest as well as a question to provide an objective.

If you, or your children, have not walked before, choose from the shorter walks for your first outings. The purpose is not simply to get from A to B but to enjoy an exploration, which may be just a steady stroll in the countryside.

Castlerigg Stone Circle

The walks are graded by length and difficulty, but few landscapes are truly flat, so even shorter walks may involve some ascent. Details are given under Route Features in the information box for each route. But the precise nature of the ground underfoot will depend on recent weather conditions. If you do set out on a walk and discover the going is harder than you expected, or the weather has deteriorated, do not be afraid to turn back. The route will always be there another day, when you are fitter or the children are more experienced or the weather is better.

Tarn Hows

Bear in mind that the countryside also changes. Landmarks may disappear, stiles may become gates, rights of way may be altered. However, with the aid of this book and its maps you should be able to enjoy many interesting family walks in the countryside.

The Lake District

For walkers the thing that is so inspiring about the Lake District is the huge choice. At one end of the scale you can enjoy a simple stroll beside a lake, through a valley or alongside a river, at the other extreme you can set off boldly to 'conquer' a particular summit, though there are no unconquered summits here! Between the two ends of this spectrum are countless permutations of possibility, enough, certainly, to last a lifetime.

Ullswater

There are over 2,225 miles (3,560km) of public footpaths and bridleways in the Lake District, and many miles of permissive pathways where the consent of the landowner enables walkers to explore where rights of way do not exist. These are the most prized recreation resource throughout the whole of the National Park and represent a chance for visitors (and residents) to enjoy the countryside and the unique quality of its landscape.

Initially, it was the waterfalls and 'viewing the set landscapes' that were the main reasons for people to come to the Lakes. But increasingly, guidebooks devoted more space to the surrounding summits as the pleasures of mountain walking became more popular. The earliest records of visitors walking on the mountains date from the end of the 18th century, but interest became particularly intensified during the early part of the 19th.

In 1823, Jonathan Otley, a Keswick guide, looked upon as the father of Lakeland geology, produced the wonderfully titled book, *A*

Castle Crag from beside the River Derwent

Concise Description of the English Lakes, The Mountains in their vicinity, And the Roads by which they may be visited; With Essays on Mineralogy and Geology, on Meteorology, the Floating Island on Derwent Lake, and the Black-Lead Mine in Borrowdale, and Map of the District. Unlike other, purely descriptive, books of the time, Otley's was the first describing walking routes through the mountains.

During the 19th century, walking was a serious and complex affair, and climbing a Lake District mountain approached in much the same way as an Alpine summit. Ponies were used to transport equipment and refreshments, and guides were hired. But it was a quantum leap for mankind when perceptions turned 'mountains' into 'fells'. Soon it was commonplace to find many of the valleys echoing to the sound of walkers as the pursuit of fell walking took on a new dimension.

In no small measure, the advancement of fell walking during the second half of the 20th century, can be attributed to the work of Alfred Wainwright, sometime Borough Treasurer of Kendal, who, over a period of 13 years, produced his classic collection of *Pictorial Guides to the Lakeland Fells.* They are unquestionably unique and amazingly skilful works of art, although as practical guides they have been replaced by a vast and well-written selection of up-to-date books by contemporary authors.

Strangely, in spite of its name, the Lake District has only one 'lake', Bassenthwaite; all the others are 'tarns', 'meres' or 'waters', though 16 of them fall within the conventional understanding of a lake. Indeed, Windermere is England's longest lake (10½ miles/17km from Waterhead to Lakeside) and Wastwater its deepest (258ft/79m).

But the lakes are only one ingredient among the many that make the landscape quality of Lakeland what it is: the fells, which, in Scafell Pike, include England's highest, the valleys or dales, and the towns and villages – almost 400 of them – all contribute to satisfy the vision of John Dower, whose report, published in 1945, augured the development of National Parks as extensive areas of 'beautiful and relatively wild country ... which should be preserved for the benefit of the nation'.

Beacon Tarn

Lakeland is a place of extremes, for not only does it boast the longest and deepest lakes in England and its highest mountains, but here, too, you'll find the steepest roads (Hardknott Pass is 33 per cent, or 1-in-3; Kirkstone and Honister are both 25 per cent, or 1-in-4). St Olaf's Church in Wasdale is claimed to be the smallest church in

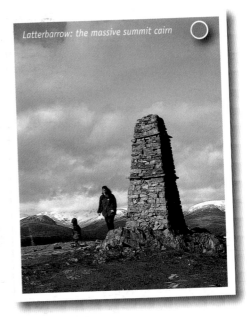

Latterbarrow: the massive summit cairn

England. In Mardale, you may see England's only golden eagles and at Santon Bridge listen to the World's Biggest Liar.

But the real beauty of the Lake District is change, from the geological shifts that only time can trace and the subtle variations wrought by the rivers and streams to the fleeting essays of light that brighten the fellsides and lowland pastures and the signature of wind across the surface of a lake. It is change, and a few indefinable qualities that brings so many visitors, in all seasons and weathers, to spend a few hours or days in the most genial of company; walking in the Lake District is an addiction that is difficult to explain, but there for all to see.

Walkers in search of solitude these days will need to know their way around the Lake District extremely well. One Monday at the beginning of February, in misty conditions on the remote Caldbeck Fells, I encountered eight other people – two fell runners and three couples; on a bitterly cold day in January, as I parked up at 08.00 at Little Town in the Newlands Valley, three other cars were ahead of me, engines warm, occupants away on the fells.

But there are countless places where you can relax peacefully listening to nature in the raw, enjoying the view, watching the Lakeland world go by – in this book, I've identified just a few.

With the introduction of 'gps enabled' walks, you will see that this book includes a list of waypoints alongside the description of the walk. We have included these so that you can enjoy the full benefits of gps should you wish to. Gps is an amazingly useful and entertaining navigational aid, and you do not need to be computer literate to enjoy it.

GPS waypoint co-ordinates add value to your walk. You will now have the extra advantage of introducing 'direction' into your walking which will enhance your leisure walking and make it safer. Use of a gps brings greater confidence and security and you will find you cover ground a lot faster should you need to.

For essential information on map reading and basic navigation, read the *Pathfinder*® *Guide Map Reading Skills* by outdoor writer, Terry Marsh (ISBN 978-0-7117-4978-8). For more information on using your gps, read the *Pathfinder*® *Guide GPS for Walkers*, by gps teacher and navigation trainer, Clive Thomas (ISBN 978-0-7117-4445-5). Both titles are available in bookshops or can be ordered online at www.totalwalking.co.uk

Newlands Valley

- Gold mine
- quiet valley
- ancient church
- ancient school

The Newlands Valley is rather less well known than most Lakeland dales, and is often used merely as a through route to Buttermere. But the valley has a fascinating legacy of industry, it is a sanctuary of the beautiful red squirrel and a perfect place to unwind and relax in relative solitude.

walk 1

Newlands Valley from Cat Bells

walk 1

START Little Town

DISTANCE 1½ miles (2.4km)

TIME 1 hour

PARKING Parking area adjacent to Chapel Bridge, Little Town

ROUTE FEATURES Fell and farm tracks; one stream crossing; some boggy ground

GPS WAYPOINTS
- ✎ NY 232 194
- Ⓐ NY 230 184
- Ⓑ NY 230 193

PUBLIC TRANSPORT None

REFRESHMENTS Teas, Low Snab Farm; pubs in Braithwaite; full facilities for all the family in Keswick

PUBLIC TOILETS None

PICNIC/PLAY AREA None

ORDNANCE SURVEY MAPS Explorer OL4 (The English Lakes – North Western area)

Leave the parking area beside Chapel Bridge and, climbing gently, walk along the lane towards Little Town. As soon as the fence on the right ends, however, leave the lane by crossing a step-stile on the right to gain a rising, stepped path to a higher and more substantial track that heads south (right) to the dale head.

Follow the track as it ambles along agreeably until, below Lowthwaite Crag, the intake wall of Low Snab Farm abruptly changes direction Ⓐ.

Turn right, with the wall, crossing a short stretch of boggy ground to a foot-bridge spanning the infant beck, and climb on the other side to another broad track, this time below a large spread of scree on the fellside. Turn right, along the track.

Copper was mined here as early as the 13th century from a vein 9¾ft (3m) thick and exceptionally rich in workable copper. The mine also produced large quantities of lead, a small amount of silver and, allegedly, a modicum of gold.

The mine's greatest period of production was in the 16th century, when Queen Elizabeth I, concerned that the country should be less dependent on foreign

Rigg Beck

supplies, made a serious attempt to exploit Britain's own resources. Ironically, it was imported German miners who largely worked Goldscope, and production was encouraged by the award of hidden subsidies in the form of waived taxes.

> ✳ The tiny chapel at Newlands was noted by **Wordsworth** in May 1826, who was struck by the appearance of the church gleaming through a veil of half-opened leaves. Much of the present building is Victorian, and the chapel retains a delightful simplicity, adjoined as it is by the old schoolroom, a place for quiet reflection.

Ore was taken by packhorse to the shores of Derwentwater, almost certainly across Chapel Bridge or its predecessor, and by way of Little Town. It was later transported to a smelter on the shores of the River Greta, at Brigham, and, having passed through Brigham, the copper then had to receive the Queen's Mark, given at the Receiving House, now the Moot Hall in Keswick.

Continue forward along the track and through a gate into the farmyard at Low Snab. A permissive path now runs out from the farm to a junction near to Newlands Chapel **B**.

? *What was the building adjoining Newlands Chapel used for?*

At the junction near the church, turn right and follow the lane back to Chapel Bridge, beyond which lies the starting point of the walk at the car park. ■

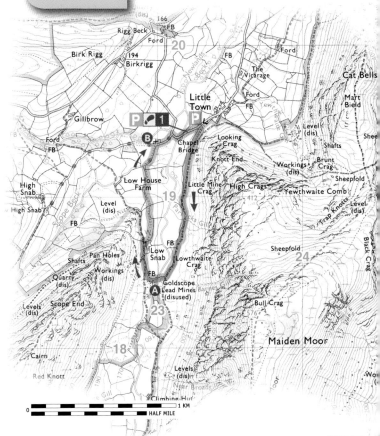

Brothers Water

- ■ Tranquil lakeside
- ■ woodland birds
- ■ ancient hall
- ■ waterside path

walk 2

Said to be named after two brothers who drowned there, Brothers Water is a small and usually tranquil lake, reflecting the surrounding fells. Its banks provide plenty of opportunity for a picnic in agreeable surroundings, enlivened especially in spring by the sound of birdsong – wood and willow warblers, chiffchaff, whitethroat, pied flycatchers, redstart and visiting cuckoos.

Brothers Water, looking towards Place Fell

walk 2

START Cow Bridge, Patterdale

DISTANCE 2½ miles (4km)

TIME 1½ hours

PARKING Cow Bridge car park

ROUTE FEATURES Woodland tracks, *slippery when wet;* lakeside path with tree roots to cross

GPS WAYPOINTS
🥾 NY 403 133
Ⓐ NY 398 120
Ⓑ NY 403 119

PUBLIC TRANSPORT None

REFRESHMENTS Brothers Water Inn, and in Patterdale

PUBLIC TOILETS None

PICNIC/PLAY AREA None

ORDNANCE SURVEY MAPS Explorer OL5 (The English Lakes – North Eastern area)

🥾 Leave the car park and cross the nearby bridge spanning Goldrill Beck, and turn left through a gate giving onto a broad, stony track. The track, never far from water, runs along the bottom edge of well-established woodland in which oak and beech predominate.

Gradually, the path rises gently, away from the water's edge, and, beyond the southern end of the lake, continues above broad alluvial pastures to reach Hartsop Hall Farm Ⓐ and Dovedale Cottage.

Follow the track past the farm and, ignoring paths going off to the right, swing round to the left, in front of the hall, and then follow a track, right, over a cattle-grid and walk along a level track towards a caravan and camping site at Sykeside Farm Ⓑ.

> **Hartsop Hall** is a working farm, built originally in the 16th century, though it has been extensively rebuilt and altered since. It was formerly the home of the de Lancasters, and later of Sir John Lowther, who became the first Viscount Lonsdale at the end of the 17th century. When the hall was extended in the 18th century, it was built across an ancient right of way, a right which at least one dalesman insisted on exercising, by walking through the hall.

Hartsop – cottage with spinning gallery

Continue through the site on a surfaced track, and go past the shop and farm buildings, bearing left at a Y-junction near the Brothers Water Hotel. Follow a driveway until, just as it reaches the road, leave it for a gate on the left giving on to a permissive path signposted for Brothers Water.

? How many different species of birds can you spot in the woodland along the first part of this walk?

Initially the path hugs the road wall, and soon reaches a gap where, for a few strides, it adjoins the road. Then it descends to the shoreline of Brothers Water. At various spots here the shoreline would be an ideal place for a picnic.

Gradually the path leaves the waterside and rises to a gate giving access to the road. Turn left and cross to a footpath opposite, and follow the road back to the Cow Bridge car park at the start of the walk.

Tarn Hows
by Tom Gill

- Attractive waterfalls
- glorious scenery
- upland tarn
- woodland wildlife

walk 3

Enormously popular, and deservedly so, Tarn Hows may be approached from numerous directions, but this walk offers an ascent through delightful oak woodland turning to birch in the higher reaches. Attractive waterfalls enliven a route already rich in wildlife interest, especially in spring.

Tarn Hows

walk 3

START Glen Mary Bridge, Tilberthwaite

DISTANCE 1½ miles (2.4km)

TIME 1 hour

PARKING Parking area at the foot of Tom Gill

ROUTE FEATURES Woodland paths; tarnside track

GPS WAYPOINTS
SD 321 998
Ⓐ SD 324 999
Ⓑ SD 327 998
Ⓒ SD 333 999

PUBLIC TRANSPORT Daily bus services to Tom Gill, and seasonal National Trust 'Tarn Hows Tourer'

REFRESHMENTS Coniston

PUBLIC TOILETS Coniston; none en route

PICNIC/PLAY AREA none

ORDNANCE SURVEY MAPS Explorer OL7 (The English Lakes – South Eastern area)

Start from the parking area at the foot of Tom Gill, and cross the nearby footbridge, turning right through a gate and ascending a steadily rising track alongside the stream.

The path, obvious all the way, passes a few low cascades as it goes up through predominantly oak woodland, but higher up it meets some more substantial falls Ⓐ with the path being signposted along a ledge above the stream.

> Although still known as **Tom Gill**, poet John Ruskin, who lived above the shores of Coniston Water at **Brantwood,** renamed Tom Gill as Glen Mary, which explains the name of the bridge at the foot of the stream.

Above the falls a kissing-gate gives into the upper woodland, now mainly birch. The path ascends the whole time but at an easy angle, and eventually pops out onto a broad and level track at the edge of Tarn Hows.

Ⓑ Turn left and follow the main track all the way round Tarn Hows, ignoring branching paths on the left.

On the far side of the tarn, when the track forks Ⓒ, take the lower, right-hand

Tom Gill

Tarn Hows

? *Is Tarn Hows a real lake?*

branch, continuing parallel to the shoreline (signposted for Coniston and Yewdale).

The track forks again just before reaching a road. Branch right, and follow a gently descending path back to the top of Tom Gill. Turn left, and retrace the upward route, back to the foot of Tom Gill and the starting point.

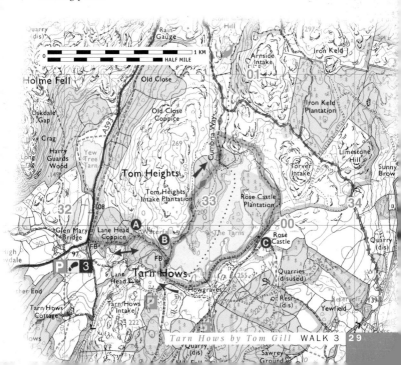

Barrow

- Mountain vista
- heathland views
- pretty village
- good pubs

The diminutive Barrow occupies an enviable position on the edge of the Newlands Valley, with a fine view from its summit ridge, overlooking the Vale of Keswick. A full frontal assault on the fell is the normal line of ascent, but this walk makes a less demanding approach before reaching the top of the fell and its 'surprise' view. A clear day is advised.

walk 4

Barrow from Coledale Beck

START Braithwaite

DISTANCE 3½ miles (5.6km)

TIME 2 hours

PARKING Parking area on Whinlatter road, above the village

ROUTE FEATURES Steadily rising fell path; rocky ridge and long grassy descent

GPS WAYPOINTS

- 📝 NY 227 237
- Ⓐ NY 230 235
- Ⓑ NY 223 223
- Ⓒ NY 233 230

PUBLIC TRANSPORT Daily bus services to Braithwaite

REFRESHMENTS Braithwaite has a couple of family friendly pubs; otherwise Keswick has a full range of facilities

PUBLIC TOILETS Braithwaite (on road between village and main road)

PICNIC/PLAY AREA None

ORDNANCE SURVEY MAPS Explorer OL4 (The English Lakes – North Western area)

The village of **Braithwaite** is where the renowned Cumberland Pencil Company was formed in 1868, before moving to its site in Keswick 30 years later when the buildings burned down. Braithwaite today is a quiet place with few residents employed locally, but in the past it had more than 1,000 inhabitants and its own coterie of tradespeople – butcher, baker, blacksmiths, millers, shoemaker, grocer, joiners and builders – and was closely associated with the village of Thornthwaite to the north.

Leave the car park and turn right to go down the road into Braithwaite. Take the first road on the right, crossing a stone bridge (High Bridge), and bear right, past Braithwaite Common – where there used to be a flour mill – and the Methodist church. Then leave the surfaced lane, on the left, for a brief stony track to the Coledale Inn, re-joining the surfaced lane beside the inn Ⓐ.

? *Near the start of this walk you pass Braithwaite Common. Why do you think it was called a 'common'?*

Go forward along the lane, passing in front of the inn, and curving round to ascend gently towards High Coledale Farm. At a gate the surfacing ends, and a rough track continues beyond across open country, flanked by bracken.

The track rises steadily above the surprisingly deep ravine of Barrow Gill, and then moving away from the gill, becomes a broad grassy track, now with Grisedale Pike in view on the right. Outerside also comes into view ahead, to the right of the pyramidal Stile End.

⁂ The **Coledale Inn** is clearly named after the valley that runs into the hillsides behind it, while the village's only other pub, the **Royal Oak**, commemorates Charles II who, to escape pursuing Roundheads, hid in an oak tree at Boscobel, near Shifnal in Shropshire, following the Battle of Worcester in 1651.

At the foot of Stile End the path forks **B**. Stay on the more pronounced track, branching left to pursue a gently rising path to the hause (Barrow Door) between Stile End and Barrow.

At Barrow Door, go left on a clear path climbing onto Barrow through heather and low rock outcrops. The stony path rises easily and soon reaches the top of Barrow, which has a grandstand and unrivalled view of the northern fells, the north-western fells, Newlands Valley, Derwent Water and the long line of the Dodds and Helvellyn ranges. It comes as a surprise that such a modest fell can prove to be such an excellent vantage point, and this alone makes this walk especially worthwhile.

Continue across the top of Barrow and begin descending on a rocky path. Lower down the path becomes broad and grassy, through bracken, and is a delight to walk, though it can be slippery when wet. Halfway down the ridge there is a small dip, a miniature pass, close by which there are old mine workings.

When you reach the bottom of the path from Barrow (low sign-post nearby) **C**, go left on a grassy track descending to a gate at a wall end. Through the gate walk ahead to Braithwaite Lodge Farm, and then follow its access track which leads out into the village of Braithwaite.

As you meet the village lane, turn left, and then left again immediately before hump-backed Low Bridge in the village centre. Walk beside Coledale Beck, and soon bear right, near a post box, to rejoin the outward route at Braithwaite Common. Over High Bridge, turn left and go back up the road to the start.

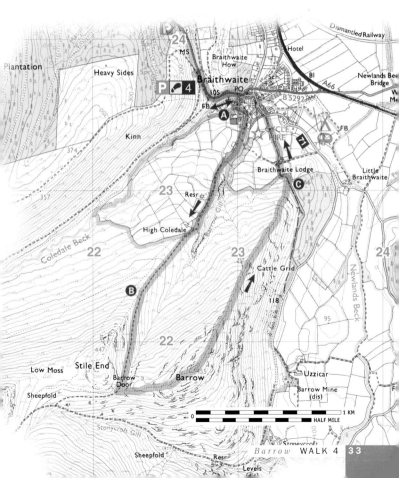

Whinlatter Forest

■ **Lovely views**   ■ **forest trails**
■ **woodland wildlife**   ■ **scent of pine**

walk 5

The great spread of Thornthwaite Forest, part of the larger Whinlatter Forest, climbs to the lovely viewpoint of Lord's Seat, too distant a prospect for this walk, but typical of the many viewpoints that occur throughout the forest, offering cameo glimpses of soaring fells and lush valleys.

Whinlatter Forest in winter

START Whinlatter Visitor Centre

DISTANCE 1½ miles (2.4km)

TIME 1 hour

PARKING Whinlatter Visitor Centre (Pay and Display)

ROUTE FEATURES Steep forest paths and tracks

GPS WAYPOINTS

🥾 NY 207 245

PUBLIC TRANSPORT Daily bus service, April–October, to Whinlatter Visitor Centre from Keswick, Buttermere and Borrowdale

REFRESHMENTS Whinlatter Visitor Centre

PUBLIC TOILETS Whinlatter Visitor Centre

PICNIC/PLAY AREA None

ORDNANCE SURVEY MAPS Explorer OL4 (The English Lakes – North Western area)

🥾 Leave the car park by walking up to the visitor centre, and there turn left onto a track (signposted 'Trails'), turning right a few strides later (also signposted 'Trails') onto a rising gravel path. Go up past a red, blue and green waymark.

At a path T-junction, turn right, still following the red, blue and green trail. Shortly, at another junction, keep left to reach a three-way junction, at a signboard on the left bearing the representation of a deer. Here, turn left, climbing energetically.

At the next junction, when the track forks, bear right, climbing steeply, to another sign with a heron on it. Here, as the track forks, bear left, leaving the main path, and climb to meet a forest trail at a welcome bench, from which there is a view across the valley to Grisedale Pike and Hobcarton End.

From the bench take the right-hand one of four possible tracks, and descend to a green waymark about 40 yds distant. At the waymark, leave the main track by turning right onto a constructed pathway into the forest, which soon starts to descend steeply.

The descending path leads down to another clearing/viewing area, with a sign nearby bearing a snail. The viewing takes in the

? **What are the main types of trees you will find in Whinlatter Forest?**

Helvellyn range and Hospital Fell, a northerly continuation of Grisedale Pike.

Hospital Fell is named after an isolation hospital for sailors with tuberculosis.

From the viewing area, keep left, descending on a red and blue trail. This leads down to meet a broad, forest trail. Turn left, climbing gently to a red and blue waymark about 100 yds away. At the waymark, leave the main trail, and descend, right, on the blue trail.

Forest Trail, Whinlatter

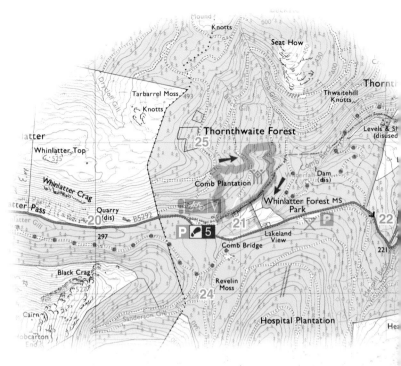

The view across to Helvellyn overlooks the **Vale of Keswick**, a lush, low-lying area with an extensive pattern of fields, hedgerows, trees and small woods that shelter the market town of Keswick. This valley pattern contrasts with the high open fells behind, among which Helvellyn is one of Lakeland's small number of summits to exceed 3,000ft (915m).

The blue trail goes down agreeably amid, in spring, much birdsong, to meet another main forest track, at which turn right, bringing you now onto the red trail, a broad forest track.

The descending track leads to a junction with a signpost numbered 14 nearby. Here, turn right to remain on the broad trail, which reunites the red and blue trails, and eventually leads back to the visitor centre and the starting point of the walk. ■

Loughrigg Tarn

- White-water falls
- walled tracks
- lakeside views
- riverside path

Beyond a brief pull up a brackeny slope, this walk is delightful, wandering around Loughrigg Tarn before heading down to the valley to finish alongside the foaming River Brathay. There are viewing platforms for those who want a closer look at the splendid Skelwith Force, though young children should not be allowed to use them unattended.

walk 6

Loughrigg Tarn

START Silverthwaite

DISTANCE 2¾ miles (4.5km)

TIME 1½ hours

PARKING Silverthwaite parking area (Pay and Display)

ROUTE FEATURES Narrow paths through bracken; rough tracks and lanes

GPS WAYPOINTS

🖉 NY 340 037
Ⓐ NY 341 042
Ⓑ NY 345 045
Ⓒ NY 346 040
Ⓓ NY 343 034

PUBLIC TRANSPORT Daily bus service between Ambleside and Langdale

REFRESHMENTS Pub at Skelwith Bridge and café in Kirkstone Galleries

PUBLIC TOILETS None

PICNIC/PLAY AREA None

ORDNANCE SURVEY MAPS Explorer OL7 (The English Lakes – South Eastern area)

From the car park a permissive path runs up alongside the garden wall of Silverthwaite Cottage. It climbs steeply for a short while, and affords a fine view of the Langdale Pikes.

At a cross-path, go forward and follow an obvious route around the north-western shoulder of Little Loughrigg to reach a cottage (Crag Head) Ⓐ, and gain your first view of Loughrigg Tarn.

Descend to the left of the cottage, immediately bearing left onto a vehicle access track which leads to a surfaced lane.

Turn left for about 150 yds, and there leave the lane, at a signposted foot-path, by crossing a step-stile on the right into a sloping pasture. Head down-field on a grassy path to a ladder-stile. Over this, go forward, taking the higher of two green paths, to a gate giving onto a rough track Ⓑ.

Through the gate, turn right and follow the track to a gate beside a cottage. Through the gate, when the continuing track forks, branch right past Dillygarth Cottage, and soon reach a surfaced lane.

Turn left descending to a road junction. Turn right, soon crossing a stream near another road junction **C**.

Bear right, and continue following the road and, near the top of a rise, leave it, by turning left onto the rough track (signposted to Skelwith Bridge) to Crag Head used on the outward part of the walk.

Loughrigg Tarn was a place much-loved by Wordsworth, who, in a little-known *Epistle to Sir George Howland Beaumont*, written in 1811, describes the tarn as 'Diana's Looking-glass! … round, clear and bright as heaven'.

At Crag Head, keep forward, following a path through bracken-clad hummocks dotted with low rock outcrops, to a gate giving into the larch woodland of Neaum Crag. A gravel path leads forward to the edge of a holiday park of wooden chalets.

Keep ahead, descending on a service road, the onward route waymarked by yellow arrows. At a junction, go forward, and, immediately after a sleeping policeman, keep right of a chalet called 'Angle Tarn'.

Pass another – 'Yew Tree Tarn' – and head for a waymarked path enclosed by a low fence.

The path leads to a gate, go left on a path sandwiched between a wall and fence, which eventually gives into an open field. Keep forward, descending, and head for a kissing-gate giving onto the main road below **D**.

The falls of **Skelwith Force** make a tremendous spectacle when in spate. Here the underlying rock drops 20–30ft (6–9m) in dramatic fashion, almost invariably providing a white-water show. Metal walkways lead down to a better viewing position, though *they are not suitable for unattended children*.

Through the gate, turn left and cross the road with care, turning right at the nearby road junction, and shortly, just before Skelwith Bridge, right again alongside the River Brathay, heading for the Kirkstone Galleries. At the entrance to the galleries, bear right and walk through the workshops to a riverside path beyond.

? The falls of Skelwith Force are spectacular, but what is the name of the river?

Go along the path, passing the falls of Skelwith Force, and continuing to a gate which gives onto a large and flat pasture. Follow the main path beside the river, gradually circling round to draw level with a small knoll crowned by a stand of trees. Leave the main path here, by turning right onto a narrow path, passing to the right of the knoll and continuing to a gate giving into woodland. A gravel path now leads up through trees to the valley road, emerging directly opposite the Silverthwaite car park. Cross the road with great care. ■

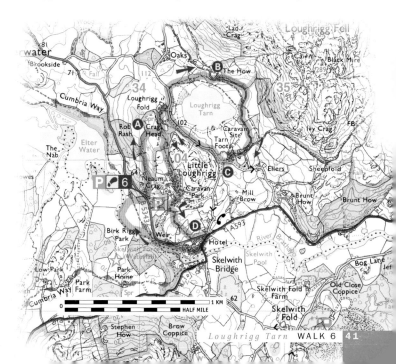

Grizedale Forest

- Woodland trails
- forest sculptures
- waterfalls
- mountain tarn

A perfect place to wander in the off-season, when the forest is less well populated, but its beauty and wildlife remain. Numerous sculptures are dotted along the trail, some offering scope for the expression of musical talent, others leaving you to scratch your head! The woodland birdlife is also impressive.

walk 7

Red Sandstone Fox, Grizedale Forest

START Grizedale Visitor Centre

DISTANCE 3 miles (4.8km)

TIME 2 hours

PARKING Grizedale Visitor Centre car park (Pay and Display)

ROUTE FEATURES Woodland tracks and stony paths

GPS WAYPOINTS
 SD 335 944
Ⓐ SD 345 952
Ⓑ SD 346 944

PUBLIC TRANSPORT None, except the post bus

REFRESHMENTS Grizedale Tea Room

PUBLIC TOILETS Adjoining visitor centre

PICNIC/PLAY AREA None

ORDNANCE SURVEY MAPS Explorer OL7 (The English Lakes – South Eastern area)

 Begin by walking past the Guardian of the Forest to the main road. Turn right for a short distance, taking care against approaching traffic and, at the first building on the left, cross the road and turn left onto a rising stony path. This is an unclassified road, and sometimes used by off-road vehicles: take great care should any approach.

Continue climbing, passing a few interesting sculptings – a quarry structure, larch wave seat and blind wall – on the way, with conditions underfoot improving gradually. The ascending track eventually merges with a broad forest trail. Keep right, and follow the trail to a T-junction.

At the junction, turn left, and continue with the trail, rising to a prominent Red Sandstone Fox Ⓐ. Here the trail forks. Branch right, climbing gently, and keep an eye open for a 'Feathersaurus' among the trees!

Continue following the green and white trails for some distance until they fork at an obvious Y-junction. At this point, turn left onto a narrow forest path that leads to hidden Grizedale Tarn Ⓑ. Then return to the main route.

Guardian of the forest, Grizedale

Keep following the white trail now, which shortly leaves the main forest trail for a narrower, stony path. The path descends to a stream, crossed on wooden 'stepping stones'.

Eventually the path goes down steps to meet another broad forest trail. Turn left, and when the white trail leaves this main track, branch right onto it, now descending again on a narrow stony path.

When the white trail merges with the blue trail, take the lower of two paths (though it matters little which path is taken, except that the lower route has the advantage in that it visits a number of woodland works of art).

Follow the blue trail to the new Education Centre and out across a car park to a road crossing point giving back into the grounds of the Visitor Centre to conclude the walk. ■

The blue trail is known as the **Ridding Wood Trail**, and is surfaced throughout. It contains 20 pieces of contemporary forest sculpture, most of which are encountered in the final stages of this walk. This stretch will appeal especially to young children, for there is ample opportunity for musical expression here, concealed animals in the undergrowth to find, marimbas on which to play a tune, a buzzing hive and shadow faces in the forest – and there are quite a few places for mums and dads to relax, too.

? *Can you find the 'Feathersaurus' hiding among the trees?*

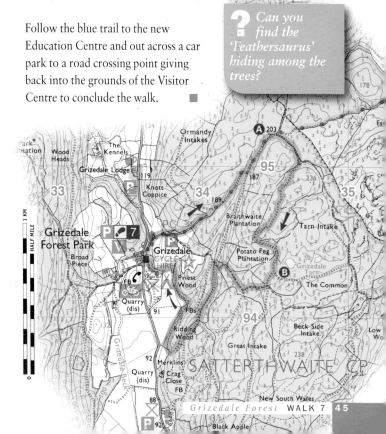

Latterbarrow

- Massive cairn
- stunning views
- flora and fauna
- woodland trail

A splendid panorama is the reward for anyone who climbs Latterbarrow. This approach takes advantage of an old bridleway across the northern slopes of Claife Heights, before swinging back to visit this popular summit.

walk 8

A view over Windermere

walk **8**

START Hawkshead

DISTANCE 3$\frac{1}{2}$ miles (5.6km)

TIME 2 hours

PARKING Hawkshead main car park (Pay and Display)

ROUTE FEATURES Good paths and tracks; muddy woodland trails; some stiles to cross

GPS WAYPOINTS

SD 353 981
Ⓐ SD 359 986
Ⓑ SD 371 985
Ⓒ SD 367 991

PUBLIC TRANSPORT Daily and seasonal bus services to Hawkshead from Ambleside and Coniston

REFRESHMENTS Hawkshead has numerous family-friendly pubs and cafés

PUBLIC TOILETS Adjoining car park

PICNIC/PLAY AREA None

ORDNANCE SURVEY MAPS Explorer OL7 (The English Lakes – South Eastern area)

The tiny hamlet of **Colthouse** seems a peaceful place, as indeed it is, overshadowed by the glitzy (by comparison) glamour of nearby Hawkshead. But Colthouse was one of the remote communities visited by George Fox in 1653, following which the hamlet became an important Quaker centre – it still has a Friends' Meeting House.

Another claim to fame is that William Wordsworth lodged here, while attending school in the village of Hawkshead.

Leave the village car park by its vehicular entrance, turn right to a T-junction and then left onto the Sawrey road. At the first junction, branch left along a narrow lane (signposted to Wray and Wray Castle). Follow the lane to Colthouse, taking care against approaching traffic, in the absence of roadside footpaths.

Pass through this pleasant hamlet and continue northwards for about 250 yds beyond the last buildings to a signposted bridleway on the right, opposite the entrance to Gillbank Ⓐ. Leave the road here, turning acutely right, through a gate onto a rising stony track. After a few yards, when the track forks, branch right. The ongoing track, climbing steadily throughout, continues for quite some distance as it crosses the wooded landscape between Latterbarrow and Colthouse

Heights for a little over one mile (1.6km), for the most part in and out of mixed woodland. There are a few branching tracks, but the main line is obvious, following a course that is roughly east.

As a viewpoint, the top of **Latterbarrow** is as good as any in Lakeland, especially so northwards across Ambleside at the head of Windermere and the ring of summits flanking Fairfield.

At a wall corner **B**, pass through a gate and onto a stony track at a forest boundary to a wall gap with a three-way signpost nearby. Here turn left on a clear path across a large area that has been storm damaged and cleared. On the far side, a stepped path leads up to another wall gap. Through the gap, turn right beside the wall and shortly swing left, once more across cleared ground, following a path that eventually leads back into forest. A path now leads along the forest boundary to a step-stile in a corner.

Over the stile turn sharply right to ascend Latterbarrow on a steadily rising track that leads directly to the enormous monument crowning the summit **C**.

From the summit take a direct line from the top of the fell – a grassy path – aiming for the distant village of Hawkshead to the south-west. Lower down the path joins another, and leads down to a country lane. Turn left for about 50 yds and then right into Loanthwaite Lane, where care is needed against approaching traffic.

? *Can you guess the height of the obelisk on the top of Latterbarrow?*

After a little under ¹⁄₂ mile, near farm buildings, take the second of two signposted footpaths close together on the left (for Hawkshead), and use this to follow a surfaced route through meadows to reach Scar House Lane, in reality an enclosed, rough track.

Turn left, and very soon go right into another meadow, with Hawkshead plainly visible ahead. The continuing path leads unerringly back towards Hawkshead. At the first of the cottages on the edge of the village, turn right over a bridge spanning a stream, and go along an enclosed path that curves around buildings and eventually emerges onto a main road.

Cross the road, continuing ahead on cobbles past attractive cottages and through an archway to arrive at the rear of the Kings Arms Hotel in the Square, which is entered via an archway.

William Wordsworth attended grammar school here from 1779 until 1787, when he went to St John's College, Cambridge. The village, in

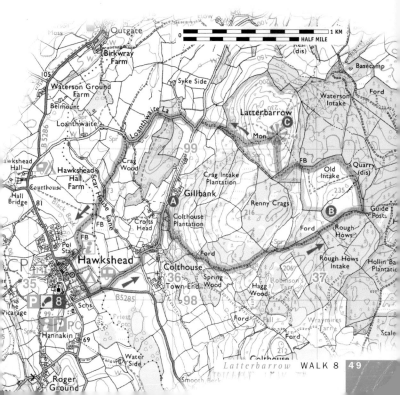

Latterbarrow: the massive summit cairn

spite of today's tourist trappings, has an air of peace and oneness with nature that would surely have impressed itself on the young boy's mind.

The village is also associated with Beatrix Potter, who lived only a few miles away at Hill Top Farm, near Sawrey, for it was here that her husband, solicitor William Heelis, had his office, which is now the Beatrix Potter Gallery.

Turn left and follow the road out of the village, to reach the turning into the car park in Hawkshead, back at the starting point of the walk.

Orrest Head
and Allen Knott

■ Iron Age hillfort ■ outstanding view
■ superb scenery ■ interesting tree

For all its modest height, Orrest Head provides one of the finest panoramas in Lakeland, rising only a short distance from the centre of Windermere. While walkers can easily return from the summit, this walk ventures farther, across farmland to Allen Knott, site of an Iron Age hillfort.

walk 9

Windermere from Allen Knot

walk 9

START Windermere (near station)

DISTANCE 4½ miles (7.2km)

TIME 2 hours

PARKING Lay-by near Windermere Hotel, on A591

ROUTE FEATURES Woodland paths; farm tracks and fields

GPS WAYPOINTS

🔖 SD 413 987
Ⓐ SD 414 993
Ⓑ NY 417 004
Ⓒ NY 413 010
Ⓓ NY 413 013
Ⓔ NY 411 000
Ⓕ SD 413 997

PUBLIC TRANSPORT Rail and bus services to Windermere

REFRESHMENTS Windermere has numerous pubs and cafés

PUBLIC TOILETS Adjoining Windermere station

PICNIC/PLAY AREA None

ORDNANCE SURVEY MAPS Explorer OL7 (The English Lakes – South Eastern area)

🔖 Directly opposite the National Westminster Bank on the main road through Windermere (A591), take the signposted path (a surfaced lane) for Orrest Head. The lane climbs initially quite steeply through light, mixed woodland, winding ever upwards. At the end of the surfaced lane, go forward onto a rough track. When the track forks at a bench, branch right.

Where the track swings round to run alongside a wall on the left, leave it and continue on a gently rising path beside the wall. The path leads to a kissing-gate, beyond which a stepped track rises onto the summit of Orrest Head Ⓐ.

From the top of Orrest Head set off roughly northwards, aiming for a conspicuous group of white farm buildings close by a small tarn below. A grassy path drops to a through-stile in a wall corner

> ✱ **Orrest Head** is a justly famous and splendid viewpoint, providing a panorama that embraces the Coniston Fells, the Langdales and the length of Windermere. The top of this little fell, according to Lakeland writer Harriet Martineau, used to be the residence of Josiah Brown, 'who amused himself ... with welcoming beggars, whom he supplied with meat and lodging'. He called them his 'jolly companions'.

beside a gate and continues descending, crossing a sloping field before running beside a wall and striking across a field punctuated by low rock outcrops, eventually to reach a back lane.

? *From the summit of Orrest Head, how many of the fells on the other side of Windermere can you name?*

Go right and about 200 yds farther on leave the road over a through-stile onto a path (signposted to Far Orrest). Keep to the right-hand field edge to a kissing-gate, cross a small enclosure to another gate, beyond which lies a small copse. This in turn gives into a larger field. Head forward to a wall corner, where a stile accesses the next field.

Follow the right-hand field margin, heading for a distant ladder-stile, and passing a lovely pollarded ash tree **B** on the way.

Over the ladder-stile, cross the ensuing field half-right aiming for distant farm buildings. After another ladder-stile, continue towards the farm buildings on a vehicle track that leads to a kissing-gate. Go through this and another nearby, then turn left along a field edge, passing the farm buildings and then turning through another gate giving onto a walled track.

Turn right along the track, and at its end keep forward beside a wall across the base of high ground, Allen Knott **C**, on the right.

The continuing path leads to a gate at a wall corner. Through this keep forward, climbing gently on a grassy track before descending to a surfaced lane **D**.

* **Pollarding** involves cutting a tree 8–12ft (2–4m) above ground, and allowing it to grow again to produce successive crops of wood. Ash was once valued for its strength and elasticity, making it ideal for tool handles and oars, but it is more usual to see ash coppiced (cut nearer the ground) than as a pollard.

At the lane, turn left, and, taking care against approaching traffic, follow the road. When it forks, branch left and descend to a signposted access for Far Orrest Farm, on the left.

Turn onto the access lane, cross a cattle-grid and, when the lane forks, branch left and continue up to Far Orrest Farm. Keep left in front of the buildings to a couple of wide gates. Cross a step-stile on the right (signposted 'Windermere via Crosses') and a farm compound, and then walk out through a gate and along a vehicle track across two fields.

In the second field, the track runs beside a wall, but when it swings left, leave it at a stile and gate in a wall corner. Climb beside a wall, soon reaching more level ground. After a ladder-stile/gate, continue on the track beyond eventually emerging at cottages and going forward to a lane **E**.

Turn left and pass Crosses Cottage, and follow the lane to the next farm (Causeway). Opposite the farm entrance, turn right, through a gate and onto a walled track. When the track enters an open field, keep forward beside a wall.

As the ongoing track moves away from the wall **F**, stay with it, climbing to a distant ladder-stile/gate. Over this, keep right alongside a wall, continuing on a terraced green path with lovely views.

The path soon descends to a through-stile beside a gate, and gives into woodland. Almost immediately bear right on a descending track. When the track forks, bear right between walls. At a path

T-junction, turn left alongside a high wall. The descending path finally emerges on the Orrest Head road, a short distance from the main road (A591) and the starting point.

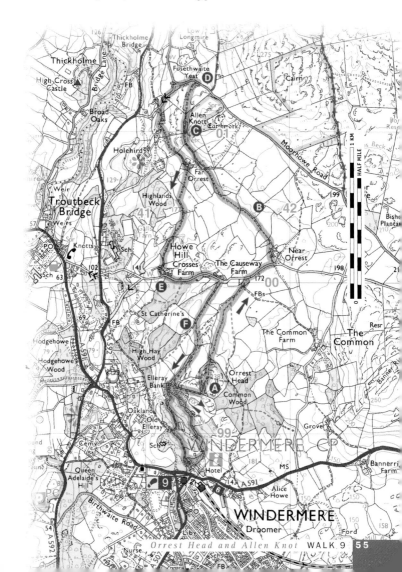

Buttermere

- ■ Secret tunnels
- ■ woodland birds
- ■ lakeside paths
- ■ glorious views

This simple tour of Buttermere is one of the most popular short walks in Lakeland, suitable for any season. The first part wanders along the base of Burtness Wood, often alive with birdsong, and provides stunning views up the valley. The return leg continues to hug the shoreline, before breaking away as it approaches the village.

walk 10

The head of Buttermere Valley

START Buttermere village

DISTANCE 4½ miles (7.2km)

TIME 2½ hours

PARKING Car park at rear of Bridge Hotel (seasonal charges)

ROUTE FEATURES Good paths throughout; a little road walking

GPS WAYPOINTS
- 🖊 NY 174 169
- Ⓐ NY 172 163
- Ⓑ NY 194 149
- Ⓒ NY 186 157

PUBLIC TRANSPORT Daily bus services (April–October) from Keswick, Whinlatter and Borrowdale

REFRESHMENTS Two pubs at Buttermere (both welcome children) and a café

PUBLIC TOILETS Adjoining car park

PICNIC/PLAY AREA None

ORDNANCE SURVEY MAPS Explorer OL4 (The English Lakes – North Western area)

The **Fish Hotel** is renowned for the story of Mary Robinson, the Maid of Buttermere, who lived and worked at the hotel. Her story was brought to fame at the turn of the 18th century. She was later wooed by, and eventually married, John Hadfield, who turned out to be an impostor and who was later hanged at Carlisle for forgery.

🖊 Leave the car park and turn right, around the Fish Hotel to follow a broad track through gates.

Ignore the signposted route to Scale Force, continue along the broad track towards the lake's edge, then follow the line of a hedgerow to a bridge at Buttermere Dubs Ⓐ.

Cross the bridge and go through a gate in a wall at the foot of Burtness Wood. Turn left on a track through the woodland that roughly follows the shoreline of the lake, finally emerging from Burtness Wood near Horse Close, where a bridge spans Comb Beck.

Keep on along the path to reach a wall leading to a sheepfold and a gate. Go left through the gate, cross Warnscale Beck and press on to Gatesgarth Farm Ⓑ.

At the farm take the gate marked 'Lakeside Path', and follow signs to reach the valley

The village of Buttermere

road. A short stretch of road walking, left on the B5289, now follows, along which there are no pathways.

As the road bends left, leave it for a footpath on the left (signposted Buttermere via Lakeshore Path). The path brings you to a step-stile into a field, beyond which it never strays far from the shoreline and leads to a stand of Scots pine, near Crag Wood **C**.

> **✳** The **tunnel** was cut by employees of George Benson, a 19th-century Manchester mill owner who then owned the Hassness Estate, so that he could walk around the lake without straying too far from its shore.

> **?** *Where do you think the name 'Buttermere' comes from?*

Beyond Hassnesshow Beck, the path enters the grounds of Hassness, where a rocky path, enclosed by trees, leads to a kissing-gate. Here a path has been cut into the crag, where it plunges into the lake below, and the path disappears into a short and dripping tunnel.

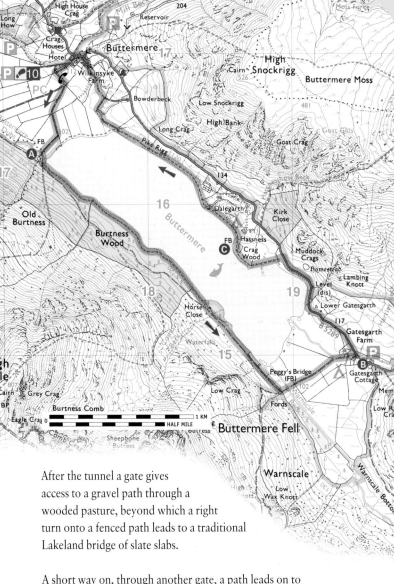

After the tunnel a gate gives
access to a gravel path through a
wooded pasture, beyond which a right
turn onto a fenced path leads to a traditional
Lakeland bridge of slate slabs.

A short way on, through another gate, a path leads on to
Wilkinsyke Farm, and finally an easy walk out to the road, just a
little way above the starting point at the Bridge Hotel.

Rydal Water

■ Wordsworth home   ■ coffin stone

■ waterfall   ■ lake and riverside

walk 11

This easy walk around Rydal Water is immensely popular at all times of year, and a simple route to follow. Such uphill walking as there is only serves to provide superb vantage points from which to appreciate the loveliness that is Rydal.

Rydal Water

walk 11

START White Moss
Common

DISTANCE 3½ miles (5.6km)

TIME 2 hours

PARKING White Moss
Common (Pay and
Display)

ROUTE FEATURES Riverside
paths; fell tracks and
fields; rocky shoulder

GPS WAYPOINTS
🖊 NY 348 065
Ⓐ NY 344 059
Ⓑ NY 359 060
Ⓒ NY 351 068

PUBLIC TRANSPORT Daily
and seasonal bus
services stop at White
Moss Common

REFRESHMENTS Both Rydal
and nearby Grasmere
have family-friendly pubs

PUBLIC TOILETS On White
Moss Common (to the left)

PICNIC/PLAY AREA none

ORDNANCE SURVEY MAPS
Explorer OL7 (The English
Lakes – South Eastern
area)

🖊 Begin from White Moss Common car
park and cross the road with care to a
descending stepped path opposite onto
White Moss Common. At the bottom of the
steps take a path bearing right beside the
River Rothay.

Ignore a river footbridge, but keep on
through a gate into another pasture and
progressing through gates eventually enter
light woodland.

Within the woodland the path immediately
forks. Branch left, climbing a little and
continue to a second footbridge, spanning
the outflow of Grasmere Ⓐ.

Cross the bridge and go up steps
immediately facing. Turn left onto a higher
path climbing to run alongside an intake
wall and then on to meet a bridleway (blue
waymark).

At this point the bridleway descends left
between a fence and wall. Lower down a
few stepping-stones take the route across an
in-flowing stream beyond which it
continues beside a wall. The path
eventually descends to pass along the
shoreline of Rydal Water, and to cross a
*low, rocky shoulder at the water's edge, on
which care is needed.*

B Towards the far end of Rydal Water, at a wall corner, the path forks. Branch left, staying along the edge of the lake, to a metal kissing-gate giving into Rydal Woods.

? *Behind the church at Rydal is Dora's Field. Who was Dora?*

Follow the continuing path through the woods, leaving at another kissing-gate. The path leads to a footbridge spanning the Rothay. On the other side, go up to meet the main road. Cross the road with care to the footpath opposite, turning right.

At the first road junction, turn left on an ascending road to Rydal Mount, passing the delightful Church of St Mary.
The Church of St Mary was built during the reign of George IV, of simple construction, with a tower, nave and chancel. William Wordsworth helped to choose the site for the church, but seems not to have been too impressed with the finished product.

Rydal Mount was home to Wordsworth and his family from 1813 until his death in 1850. Socially the house was a significant step up for the poet, putting him on calling terms with the local gentry.

Continue past Rydal Mount, behind which turn left onto a bridleway (signposted for Grasmere). A few strides on, go left through a gate onto a rough stony track that eventually breaks out into light woodland cover. The continuing track is never in doubt, and undulates along below the steepness of Nab Scar.

Rydal is a scattered grey-stone village, and its lake was a favourite spot of the Wordsworths, who would often have a picnic on the island.

Just after a gate, near an overhead power-line, and before reaching a stream with a cottage above, descend left between walls **C** on

a broad stony path beside
the stream.

The path reaches a gate, beyond
which a broad stony track leads on
to pass a waterfall.

The track between Rydal
Mount and Grasmere is
a **corpse road**, in use for the
transfer of coffins in the days
before Rydal had its own church.

Continue out to meet the main valley road. Turn right, cross a stream
bridge and soon bear right to walk back into the White Moss
Common car park at the starting point of the walk.

Silver Bay

- Cave
- picnic areas
- old quarry
- juniper bushes

This walk above the eastern shoreline of Ullswater is one of the most dramatically beautiful walks in the Lake District combining the attractions of the lake, with its steamers and sailing boats, craggy fellsides and views into the deep, penetrating valleys to the west. The return leg is a menu of changing vistas, maintaining interest throughout.

walk 12

Ullswater

START Patterdale

DISTANCE 3½ miles (5.6km)

TIME 2 hours

PARKING Pay and Display car park opposite Patterdale Hotel

ROUTE FEATURES Bracken and juniper fell slopes to cross; rocky descent to Silver Bay

GPS WAYPOINTS
🖊 NY 397 159
Ⓐ NY 399 162
Ⓑ NY 397 180

PUBLIC TRANSPORT All year and seasonal bus services daily to Patterdale from Windermere

REFRESHMENTS Patterdale pubs serve bar meals and welcome children

PUBLIC TOILETS En route, opposite White Lion Hotel

PICNIC/PLAY AREA Yes

ORDNANCE SURVEY MAPS Explorer OL5 (The English Lakes – North Eastern area)

🖊 Leave the car park and turn left to pass the White Lion. Take the next turning on the left, a narrow lane leading to the hamlet of Rooking.

On entering the hamlet, bear left, as if heading for Side Farm. Shortly go through a fell-gate, following a path signposted for Angle Tarn and Boredale Hause.

Begin along the path, but in just a few strides turn left and then go forward along a grassy path rising through bracken. This climbs gently through quarry spoil to a small grassy platform where the track forks Ⓐ. Here, take the higher path (on the right) which soon reaches a man-made cave, but which, *for safety's sake, should not be investigated too closely!*

The path continues its northerly course, always some distance above a lower path along which the walk is concluded. With some undulation, the continuing path presses on to a grassy saddle to the right of the conspicuous cone of Silver Crag, shrouded like the adjacent fellsides in juniper bushes.

Ⓑ Just over the saddle a short diversion is possible, climbing left on a sketchy path through juniper bushes onto Silver Crag, to savour an outstanding view across Ullswater to the fells of the Helvellyn and Fairfield ranges. Retrace your steps to return to the saddle. Continue the descent, passing a small reedy tarn before engaging a stony path that leads down to a prominent cross-path just above Silver Bay. Turn left.

> **Silver Bay**, its sheltered beach and the adjacent craggy headland are easily reached from what is now the main path. Here is a splendid place to relax and enjoy a picnic before setting off back to Patterdale.

To return simply follow the path around Silver Crag, following its up-and-down course, in and out of small copses and around rocky ribs until finally the buildings at Side Farm are reached.

Turn right between farm buildings and follow a broad access track out to the main Patterdale road, crossing Goldrill Beck on the way.

At the main road, turn left to return to the start. ■

Patterdale

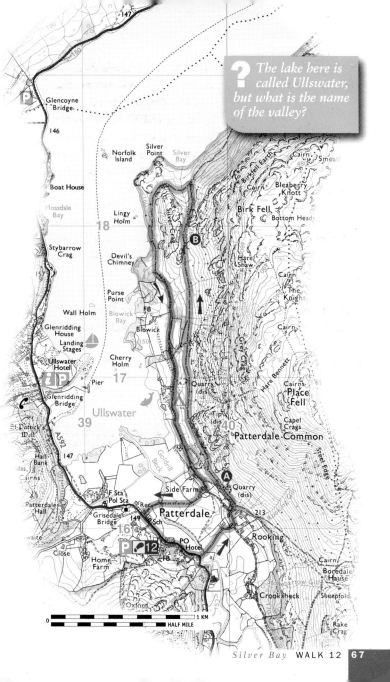

? *The lake here is called Ullswater, but what is the name of the valley?*

147

190

180

150

P

Glencoyne Bridge

146

Norfolk Island

Silver Point

Silver Bay

Cairn

Smeath

Birkfell Earth

Cairn

Bleaberry Knott

Boat House

Mossdale Bay

Lingy Holm

Birk Fell

Bottom Head

18

Stybarrow Crag

Devil's Chimney

B

Hare Shaw

157

Purse Point

Wall Holm

Cairn

The Knight

Glenridding House

Landing Stages

Ullswater Hotel

FB

Blowick Bay

Blowick

Cairn

Grey Crag

P

Glenridding Bridge

Cherry Holm

Pier

17

Quarry (dis)

Hare Bennett

Place Fell

St Patrick's Well

A592

Ullswater

39

Tip (dis)

40

Capel Crags

Hall Bank

147

Cairns

Goldrill Beck

Quarry (dis)

Patterdale Common

Steel Edge

Patterdale Hall

Side Farm

F Sta Pol Sta

A

Quarry (dis)

213

Rec

Grisedale Bridge

149

Sch

Patterdale

Rooking

16

P ⚲ 12

PO Hotel

Home Farm

Close

FB

Cairn

waite

Oxford

Crookabeck

Boredale Hause

Sheepfold

Stonebarrow Gill

Rake Crag

0   1 KM

HALF MILE

Silver Bay WALK 12 **67**

Rannerdale

- Ridge walking
- cascades
- outstanding view
- secluded valley

The descent from the top of Rannerdale Knotts is steep, slippery when wet, and goes down loose rock for a short while; *anyone feeling intimidated by this should simply retrace their steps along the ridge and down the valley – a not unpleasant compromise.* The descent should not be attempted by young or unattended children.

Cinderdale Common

START Cinderdale
Common, Rannerdale

DISTANCE 4½ miles (7.2km)

TIME 2½ hours

PARKING Cinderdale
Common

ROUTE FEATURES Good
paths; fell ridge walking;
steep, stony descent

GPS WAYPOINTS
📍 NY 162 192
Ⓐ NY 168 186
Ⓑ NY 179 177

PUBLIC TRANSPORT Daily
bus services (April –
October only) from
Keswick

REFRESHMENTS
Buttermere has two pubs
and a café

PUBLIC TOILETS None en
route

PICNIC/PLAY AREA None

ORDNANCE SURVEY MAPS
Explorer OL4 (The English
Lakes – North Western
area)

📏 Begin from the roadside parking area
on Cinderdale Common, beneath the steep
slopes of Grasmoor. Walk up beside
Cinderdale Beck for 50 yds and then cross
it at a convenient spot. Follow the broad
track on the other side, heading towards
the shapely outline of Rannerdale Knotts.

The track soon assumes a level course and
reaches a gate beyond which it continues
into the valley of Rannerdale, which has
now opened up ahead.

As the path reaches the entrance to
Rannerdale, go down to cross a footbridge
spanning Squat Beck Ⓐ.

Turn left to a gate and take to the narrow
path rising up into Rannerdale.
The story is evocatively told in *The Secret*

? *What wild flower, in
particular, is Rannerdale
famous for?*

Valley by Nicolas Size, which relates how 'It
was hopeless to try and bury great piles of
Norman dead', and how Rannerdale 'was
like a charnel house'. Today the spot where
the Normans were left is said to burst each
spring into an intensely bright carpet of
bluebells, lending some truth, perhaps, to

Omar Khayyam's notion that 'the loveliest flowers may spring from some dead Caesar's breast'.

Continue to follow the path all the way to the very highest point of the dale, a narrow col of land below the southern summit of Whiteless Pike and looking across the intervening valley to the steep slopes of Robinson.

B At the top of the dale, turn abruptly right and take to an undulating path that runs the length of the delightful ridge leading to the cairned top of Rannerdale Knotts.

> ✳ **Rannerdale,** for all its undoubted beauty, has something of a sinister history to it, for it was here, at the end of the 11th century, that the people of Buttermere ambushed and slew invading Normans, leaving their bodies to rot at the entrance to the dale.

The ridge is broad and ranks among the finest ridge walks in Lakeland, so much so that to turn tail and walk back along it is very much a tempting proposition. *If there are young children in the party, it is essential that this option be adopted in preference to attempting the steep descent to the shores of Crummock Water, which can be very intimidating for a while.*

The way down keeps initially to the right of the top of Rannerdale Knotts and soon reaches a low col between the main summit and a minor top a little lower down. Here, turn left to continue the descent, which becomes increasingly steep and leads into a loose, rocky gully where hands, feet and bottoms will be brought into play.

At the bottom of the gully, continue forward a short distance, then swing left and right through bracken with the descending path, which heads down to cross the craggy slopes above Hause Point. Continue descending, much more easily now, to reach the road. Turn right for a short distance, and turn into a parking area. Go through the parking area *(which can be used as an alternative start by anyone wanting to shorten this walk)*, and follow a wall until it becomes possible to move away from it and to turn into the entrance to Rannerdale once more. This time there is a fine view of the many low cascades that enliven Squat Beck at this point.

Recross the footbridge over Squat Beck **A** and retrace the outward route to Cinderdale Common. ■

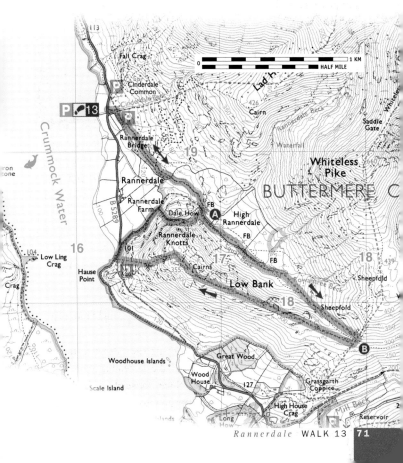

Castlerigg and Tewet Tarn

■ Prehistoric site   ■ ancient bridge
■ upland tarn   ■ old church

walk 14

Castlerigg Stone Circle is a popular place with visitors to the northern Lake District, and rightly so, its ancient stones are a great fascination. This walk starts and finishes close by them, but forms a wide loop to visit reedy Tewet Tarn and the isolated church of St John's in the Vale before trekking back across low-lying farmland.

Castlerigg Stone Circle

walk 14

START Castlerigg
Stone Circle

DISTANCE 4 miles (6.4km)

TIME 2 hours

PARKING Roadside parking
area adjoining Castlerigg

ROUTE FEATURES Back
lanes; farm fields; access
tracks; stiles and
hummocky fellsides

GPS WAYPOINTS

🖉 NY 292 237
Ⓐ NY 299 238
Ⓑ NY 304 240
Ⓒ NY 304 233
Ⓓ NY 306 225
Ⓔ NY 290 225

PUBLIC TRANSPORT None

REFRESHMENTS Keswick
has numerous family-
friendly pubs and cafés

PUBLIC TOILETS None en
route

PICNIC/PLAY AREA None

ORDNANCE SURVEY MAPS
Explorer OL4 (The English
Lakes – North Western
area)

🖉 Leave Castlerigg Stone Circle by
walking east (away from Keswick) along the
lane, but take care against approaching
traffic. The road descends round a bend
and soon reaches Goosewell Farm.

Go through a gate on the right (signposted)
and cross to another a short distance away,
then head down-field diagonally left,
aiming for a distant bridge.

Pass through another gate and cross to a
ladder-stile at a gate gap, then cross to a
gate giving onto the lane Ⓐ crossing the
Naddle Beck.

Turn right and cross the bridge. Follow the
road to a T-junction and turn right, walking
as far as the next junction on the right
(signposted Shundraw and St John's in the
Vale Church) Ⓑ.

Turn right again, following this quiet lane,
but once more taking care against
approaching traffic.

After about 350 yds, leave the lane at a five-
bar gate on the right. Through the gate,
bear right, climbing gently on a grassy
vehicle track to reach a wall gap at the top
of the field.

Through the gap continue climbing beside a wall, and later bearing away from the wall to a signpost, beyond which Tewet Tarn comes into view.

From the signpost, cross a shallow ravine, and follow an indistinct grassy path across a pasture to a through-stile to the left of a wall gap. Over this, go forward on a broad grassy track to the right of the stile, which passes close by Tewet Tarn.

Beyond the tarn the path improves and leads to a step-stile over a fence **C**. Ahead now is the rugged lump of Low Rigg, the next objective. A grassy path leads towards it, and passes just to the right of the summit.

Now the path scampers downhill to cross a wall at a through-stile, beyond which it continues through bracken, heading for a small cluster of buildings in the distance. As the buildings are approached, the path picks a way across wet ground to a through stile giving onto a surfaced lane at St John's in the Vale Church **D**. The lane was once an important thoroughfare linking the valleys east and west with their church.

Turn right, pass a Diocesan Youth Centre, and follow the lane to a distant gate. Beyond the gate a broad vehicle track descends, winding down, with widening views, to meet a surfaced lane near Sykes Farm.

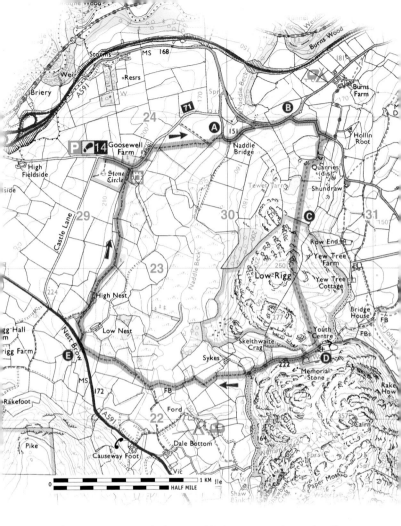

At this junction, cross the lane to a kissing-gate nearby, and walk down field, following a green path. Soon the path reaches another kissing-gate at the bottom of the pasture. In the ensuing field, head towards a gate on the right at the end of a wall (waymark). Do not go through the gate, but keep alongside the ongoing fence to another gate and fence at a wall corner.

Beyond this cross to a nearby footbridge and cross the next field on a grassy path to a distant signpost at which a vehicle track is met.

Turn right, signposted for Keswick, and walk to a five-bar gate in a wall corner. Through this continue up the right-hand field margin to a through-stile at the top. Follow a grassy track across the next field to a kissing-gate giving onto the busy A591 **E**.

Turn right, and after 50 yds, turn right again onto an access track to Low Nest Farm.

Immediately after crossing a cattle-grid, turn left through a kissing-gate, and walk up the ensuing field on a grassy path that leads to the access to High Nest Farm. Turn right and walk on to pass the farm buildings to a gate, and then keep forward on a muddy path parallel with the right-hand field margin. Keep to the field margin to reach a kissing-gate, then cross to another not far away, and repeat this in the next field.

> **Castlerigg Stone Circle** is believed to pre-date the great circles at Stonehenge and elsewhere. It is commonly regarded as one of the most superb stone circles of the many to be found in Britain. Enthusiasts believe Castlerigg to be among the earliest stone circles in Europe, though poet John Keats was not impressed, describing the stones (in *Hyperion*) as 'a dismal cirque, Of Druid stones upon a forlorn moor'.

> **?** According to the information boards, how old is Castlerigg Stone Circle?

Follow a green path across pasture, heading for a distant plantation. The path then runs past the woodland to meet a lane. Turn left here to return to the starting point of the walk. ∎

Cat Bells

■ Ridge walking
■ old road
■ outstanding view
■ rocky scrambles

Arguably the best known of the lower Lakeland fells: many a first, faltering step to fell-walking freedom was planted on the grassy slopes of Cat Bells, a summit that remains ever popular throughout the year for its outstanding views of Derwent Water, Borrowdale and the Newlands Valley.

walk 15

En route to Cat Bells

walk 15

START Hawse End

DISTANCE 3½ miles (5.6km)

HEIGHT GAIN 1,150ft (350m)

TIME 2 hours

PARKING Small wooded parking area at Hawse End

ROUTE FEATURES Steep ascent and descent; rocky outcrops

GPS WAYPOINTS

🥾 NY 247 212
Ⓐ NY 244 205
Ⓑ NY 244 192
Ⓒ NY 248 187

PUBLIC TRANSPORT Derwent ferry to Hawse End all year; bus services to Hawse End (April – October) from Keswick, Borrowdale and Buttermere

REFRESHMENTS Portinscale and Keswick

PUBLIC TOILETS None en route

PICNIC/PLAY AREA None

ORDNANCE SURVEY MAPS Explorer OL4 (The English Lakes – North Western area)

🥾 Begin from Hawse End (Hawes End on the map), where the road from Swinside and Portinscale makes a sharp zigzag before turning round the side of Cat Bells. Above the hairpin bend, at the junction for Skelgill, take a stepped path rising up the fellside.

Follow this through all its twists and turns, climbing steadily through grass and bracken to encounter a few small rocky outcrops before reaching the lower, northernmost summit of Cat Bells, sometimes called Brandlehow Ⓐ.

The onward route is never in doubt, a broad trail keeping to the centre of a grassy ridge, before rising dramatically through more rock outcrops to the cone of Cat Bells. In a few places the path moves close to the grassy slopes, which *will be slippery when wet, so care is needed until the summit is reached.* The final ascent is not so demanding as it appears when viewed end on.

The initial descent from Cat Bells involves negotiating its rocky summit ring before

? *When you stand on the summit of Cat Bells, what is the name of the next mountain to the south?*

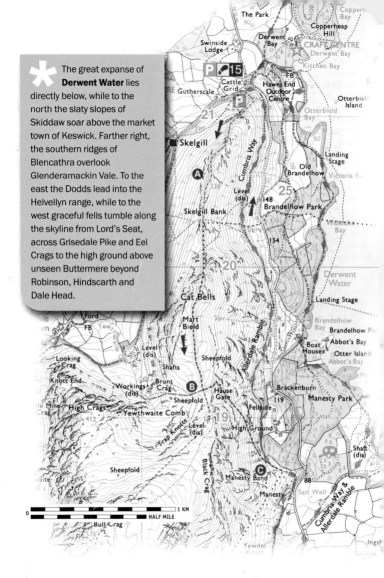

The great expanse of **Derwent Water** lies directly below, while to the north the slaty slopes of Skiddaw soar above the market town of Keswick. Farther right, the southern ridges of Blencathra overlook Glenderamackin Vale. To the east the Dodds lead into the Helvellyn range, while to the west graceful fells tumble along the skyline from Lord's Seat, across Grisedale Pike and Eel Crags to the high ground above unseen Buttermere beyond Robinson, Hindscarth and Dale Head.

descending easily to the broad col of Hause Gate **B**. Here turn left, descending a constructed pathway towards the wooded area around Manesty below.

Keep descending to meet a broad track going left along the edge of woodland **C**. (There are two earlier and higher shortcuts that meet this same track, though the higher of the two requires care in wet conditions.)

Turn left, and follow the path above woodlands and the attractively set house of Brackenburn.

Press on beyond Brackenburn, the path soon dipping to make a brief acquaintance with the road at a small quarry car park. Beyond this gap, immediately return to a gently rising path, an old road, traversing the lower slopes of Cat Bells, that will ultimately bring you back to the road at Hawse End.

Cross the road and go down a brief shortcut to a gate near a cattle-grid, from which the parking area is soon reached.

On the summit of Cat Bells with the North West fells beyond

Blawith Common and Beacon Tarn

- ■ Views of high fells
- ■ Cumbria Way
- ■ isolated tarn
- ■ ... and a mystery

Concealed high among the brackeny folds of Blawith Common, the idyllic Beacon Tarn is a perfect spot for a picnic set against the magnificent backdrop of the Coniston and Dunnerdale Fells; a real eye-opener and an ideal place to find a little solitude.

walk 16

Blawith Common

START Brown Howe, Coniston shore

DISTANCE 3½ miles (5.6km)

TIME 2½ hours

PARKING Brown Howe car park on shore of Coniston Water

ROUTE FEATURES Some busy road walking to start; brackeny fells, muddy when wet, and minor unenclosed road to finish

GPS WAYPOINTS
◢ SD 291 911
Ⓐ SD 286 901
Ⓑ SD 281 899
Ⓒ SD 275 905

PUBLIC TRANSPORT Daily bus services (Monday–Saturday, and summer Sundays) run along the A5084 from Coniston

REFRESHMENTS Pub in Torver, but otherwise Coniston has a host of family-friendly facilities

PUBLIC TOILETS Brown Howe car park

PICNIC/PLAY AREA None

ORDNANCE SURVEY MAPS Explorer OL6 (The English Lakes – South Western area)

◢ Leave the car park and turn left along the road. Cross the road and go past a road junction and, for safety (but not of necessity), shortly afterwards take to a rough track ascending, on the right, towards a disused quarry.

Just before the quarry entrance, bear left onto a grassy path through bracken. This path, roughly parallel with the road below, involves dodging below branches, and shortly leads back down to the road.

Continue along the road, with great care, until, having passed two parking areas on the left (Blawith Common), a track is reached on the right, just as the road bends left. Ⓐ The track rises steadily onto brackeny slopes.

Near overhead powerlines, the track forks Ⓑ. Branch left, still climbing. Eventually the path crosses the shoulder of Slatestone Fell and descends to a path junction, close by a wooden footbridge. Turn right. The path continues through a landscape of undulating bracken hummocks punctuated

? *When you reach Beacon Tarn, what is the name of the group of fells you can see in the distance across the tarn?*

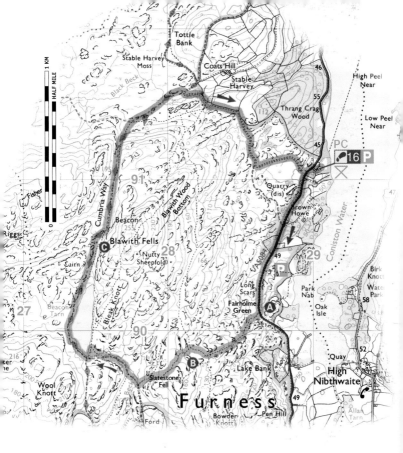

Beacon Tarn is surprisingly large, almost a lake, and is the 'Trout Tarn' of Arthur Ransome's 'Swallowdale' (*Swallows and Amazons*, 1930), in which Roger was taught how to 'guddle' trout. North-east of the tarn rises Beacon Fell, a neat craggy summit with fascinating outcrops.

by low, rock outcrops. When the path next forks, just by some stepping-stones bridging a stream, turn right, crossing the stones and walking on to the edge of Beacon Tarn, which remains concealed until the very last moment.

Speculation invariably arises among readers of Ransome's tales

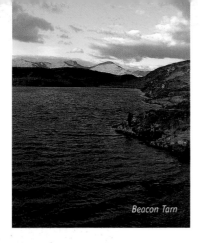
Beacon Tarn

about where, exactly, Swallowdale is. Of course, the author never disclosed his locations, but at Beacon Tarn you may be forgiven for thinking you are very close – something of a mystery, that can be resolved by reading the book itself.

At the water's edge, turn left. Across the next section numerous paths diverge, but the immediate objective is simply to walk around the tarn, keeping to an obvious path that leads the way – this is, in fact, part of the Cumbria Way, a popular Lakeland medium-distance walk.

Beyond the northerly edge of the tarn, a grassy path ascends through a gap **C** between low-lying fells, and provides outstanding views of the Coniston Fells ahead.

After the gap, the path descends steadily to pass a low-lying marshy area, and slips easily through another shallow col before moving out onto a broad expanse of mossland.

Gradually the path starts heading for the distant green cone of Coats Hill and the minor road by which the walk concludes. When the descending path forks, branch left, staying on the more prominent of the two paths.

Eventually, when the path meets the road, turn right, and follow it through an agreeable birch and ash landscape to meet the main road at a T-junction, only a short distance from the entrance to the Brown Howe car park. ■

Elterwater

- White-water falls
- nice woodland
- riverside walks
- old bridge

This delightful and easy walk meanders through farm fields and beside tarns, streams and rivers, with exquisite views of the surrounding fells. The going is nowhere difficult, and interest remains high throughout the walk.

walk 17

Slater's Bridge

walk 17

START Elterwater village

DISTANCE 5½ miles (8.9km)

TIME 3 hours

PARKING Elterwater car park, just south of the Britannia Inn, or Elterwater Common, north of the village

ROUTE FEATURES Good paths all the way; spectacular waterfalls and riverside paths

GPS WAYPOINTS

- NY 328 048
- Ⓐ NY 338 041
- Ⓑ NY 341 035
- Ⓒ NY 339 031
- Ⓓ NY 328 031
- Ⓔ NY 312 030

PUBLIC TRANSPORT Daily bus services run from Ambleside into Langdale

REFRESHMENTS Pubs at Elterwater and Skelwith Bridge, café at Kirkstone Galleries

PUBLIC TOILETS None

PICNIC/PLAY AREA None

ORDNANCE SURVEY MAPS Explorer OL7 (The English Lakes – South Eastern area)

Take the path to Skelwith (pronounced Skellith) Bridge from the river corner of the car park, a route initially requiring little description as it wanders on pleasantly to a superb resting place beside Elter Water Ⓐ. The Langdale Pikes rise across the tarn, their crags and gullies often so vividly etched you

> **?** *What kind of tree is it growing in front of the Britannia Inn in Elterwater village?*

feel you could reach out and touch them. Beyond the tarn, keep to the obvious path, passing through a gate close to the main road, and then pressing on soon to reach an attractive footbridge Ⓑ spanning the River Brathay. Cross the bridge into broad-leaved woodland, following a clear path that eventually leads round to join another, ascending from the left. Here, turn right, climbing gently through Bridge How Coppice.

At the top edge of the woodland, go through another kissing-gate and continue on an obvious stony path that soon meets a rough vehicle access track. Turn right, following the track past a group of cottages and through two metal kissing-gates. The continuing path is obvious and leads to

Colwith Force, one of Lakeland's secret waterfalls

Elterwater Park Country Guest House **C**.

Leave the buildings behind by following a waymarked path descending to a step-stile, and on to a gap-stile in a field corner. This gives onto an enclosed path, at the end of which cross to a metal kissing-gate. Follow an obvious path across a sloping field to a step-stile perched dramatically above the River Brathay.

The path that follows skims along the top of a steep drop to the river before descending an awkward path to the riverside and crossing a small enclosure to a lane. Turn right for about 80 yds, and then leave the lane, on the left, at a footpath signposted to High Park.

Cross two stiles adjoining the road and then bear immediately right on a permissive path to Colwith Force. As you approach, keep to the right of a fenced enclosure to reach a grandstand view of the falls **D**.

Retrace your steps and walk around the enclosure, climbing to cross a low shoulder high above the falls.

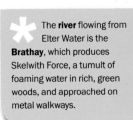

The **river** flowing from Elter Water is the **Brathay**, which produces Skelwith Force, a tumult of foaming water in rich, green woods, and approached on metal walkways.

Now, follow a woodland path, initially parallel with the river, but then moving away from it to rise to a gate in a wall. Through this, follow the continuing wall and soon turn right to walk across to High Park Farm. There turn left and go up to a lane, turning right and following the lane to Stang End, where the road zigzags between buildings.

Stay on this quiet lane to the edge of woodland and then follow a broad track round to a footbridge spanning the Brathay. Do not cross the bridge, but instead go left beside the river on a rough track until, at a kissing-gate on the right, you can leave the track to approach nearby Slater Bridge **E**.

> Set in the **stonework** of one of the buildings here is some of the handiwork of an apprentice stonemason – a homework exercise, perhaps?

Cross the bridge and keep straight ahead beside a wall on your right (ignoring gaps and diverting pathways). The path rises with the wall, and provides an outstanding view to your left of Little Langdale Tarn and Greenburndale beyond. The path leads up to a farm access. Turn left and walk out to the Little Langdale road.

Go left again and then immediately right onto a lane that after another farm degenerates into a rough, stony track.

Slater Bridge is a superb legacy of quarrying times, a cobbled, narrow construction leading to a slab bridge across the infant river.

Beyond a gate, as the track enters light woodland, keep right and continue descending, with increasing roughness underfoot, eventually to meet a lane leading out to the Elterwater road. Turn left to return to the village.

Grisedale

- Mountain views
- moraines
- waterfalls
- stunning scenery

Many visitors to Lakeland use Grisedale as a through-route or for access to the high fells of the Fairfield and Helvellyn ranges. Here it is visited for its own intrinsic qualities of pastoral pleasantness and a taste of the mountains.

walk 18

Central Grisedale

walk **18**

START Patterdale

DISTANCE 6 miles (9.7km)

TIME 3 hours

PARKING Pay and Display car park opposite Patterdale Hotel

ROUTE FEATURES Fell paths, farm tracks and rugged mountain terrain

GPS WAYPOINTS
🥾 NY 397 159
Ⓐ NY 389 155
Ⓑ NY 382 157
Ⓒ NY 359 138

PUBLIC TRANSPORT All year and seasonal bus services daily to Patterdale from Windermere

REFRESHMENTS Patterdale pubs (family-friendly); shop

PUBLIC TOILETS Opposite White Lion Hotel

PICNIC/PLAY AREA None

ORDNANCE SURVEY MAPS Explorer OL5 (The English Lakes – North Eastern area)

🥾 Turn left out of the car park and opposite the White Lion turn right onto a signposted path climbing past public toilets. At the rear of an isolated building, leave the track by turning left onto a signposted path through bracken and heather. This leads to a gate giving onto open fellside.

A path climbs rockily for a short while before descending to a kissing-gate to the left of two other gates. Through this, follow the continuing wall, then climb to a horizontal path before descending gently to cross Hag Beck on stepping-stones Ⓐ. The path continues easily, crossing the slopes of Glenamara Park and the steeper slopes below Thornhow End.

Follow the path as it runs alongside a wall bounding a pine plantation, and then maintain a level course as the wall drops away to the right. A short way on, the path rejoins a wall and then leads to a gate. Pass through this gate and continue descending beside a wall to a couple of sheepfolds. There turn right through a gate, going down-field, past a barn to a surfaced track Ⓑ.

> **?** *Many of the farm buildings along this walk have a pattern of holes high in their gable ends. What do you think they were for?*

> **Intake walls** were built as the outer limits of valley farms, and are found everywhere throughout Lakeland. But the wall at the head of Grisedale is quite stupendous, and rises crazily onto the slopes of Striding Edge. Here especially it is a lasting testimony to a skilled and dying breed of men.

Turn left and follow the track up-valley. When it swings round to access Braesteads Farm, keep ahead onto a graded track to Elmhow Farm. After Elmhow Farm, the path becomes increasingly rugged as the route penetrates to the heart of the high fells and into a harsher, mountain landscape.

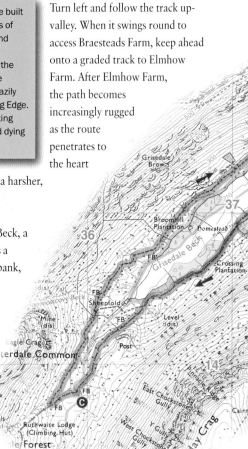

Below Nethermostcove Beck, a footbridge may be used as a shortcut to the opposite bank, but otherwise continue climbing. There is increasing ruggedness underfoot until Grisedale Beck is crossed **C**.

A rough path leads on to join a path descending from nearby Ruthwaite Lodge. At this turning point, cross another footbridge and begin the return journey.

A good path now sweeps back down the valley, giving lovely views of waterfalls not seen on the ascent, and passing through the intake wall below Nethermostcove Beck.

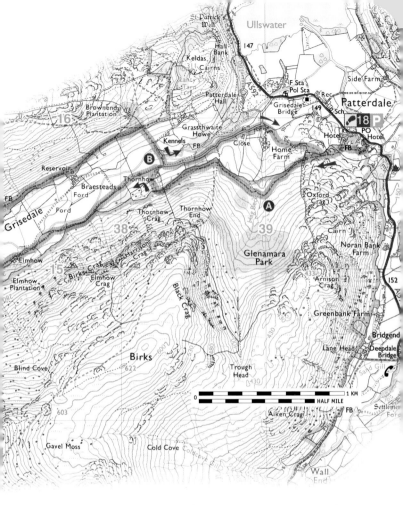

Continue following the descending path, which re-ascends briefly after passing above Braesteads Farm. Eventually it reaches a wall corner, where there are two gates. Go through the right-hand one, and down-field to a surfaced farm access below.

Keep forward to cross Grisedale Beck, now a much quieter version of its ebullient former self. At a T-junction, turn left and follow a

The view towards the head of Grisedale

surfaced lane until it makes a pronounced left turn. Here leave it by branching right onto a wide track (signposted). Shortly, leave the track at a waymark, pass through a kissing-gate, and follow a waymarked route across rough pasture to a high through-stile in a wall. Over the wall, rejoin the outward route. Turn left to follow it back to the start. ∎

The valley of **Grisedale** was fashioned along the line of a geological fault, but was once occupied by a huge glacier feeding into the main Patterdale glacier. By looking along the valley sides, a good idea can be gleaned of the depth of the glacier at this point. When the glacier retreated about 11,000 years ago, it started to deposit the heavy mountain debris it could no longer carry, and this collected into enormous piles of rubble known as moraine. Below Ruthwaite Lodge there are many examples of these hummocky moraines, remnants of that last Ice Age.

Latrigg

walk 19

- Old bobbin mill
- outstanding view
- river scenery
- old bridge

In spite of lying below the massive bulk of Skiddaw, Latrigg maintains a dominant position overlooking the market town of Keswick. The usual ascent involves continuous uphill walking, but here an approach is started along the trackbed of the former Penrith–Keswick–Cockermouth railway before slipping fairly easily onto the eastern end of Latrigg.

Ascending into Latrigg

walk 19

START Keswick (disused) railway station

DISTANCE 5 miles (8km)

TIME 3 hours

PARKING At railway station

ROUTE FEATURES Old railway trackbed, one steepish climb on country lane, grassy ridge and gradual descent

GPS WAYPOINTS

🥾 NY 272 237
Ⓐ NY 286 241
Ⓑ NY 296 251
Ⓒ NY 281 253

PUBLIC TRANSPORT Numerous daily bus services to Keswick

REFRESHMENTS Keswick town centre has numerous family-friendly pubs and cafés

PUBLIC TOILETS At start

PICNIC/PLAY AREA None

ORDNANCE SURVEY MAPS Explorer OL4 (The English Lakes – North Western area)

🥾 From the old Keswick railway station, head along the trackbed, which quickly leads away from Keswick to begin a gentle flirtation with the River Greta that continues throughout the early part of the walk.

The way forward is never in doubt, and just before the path passes beneath the elevated A66 an interesting milepost is encountered, one of 1,000 funded by the Royal Bank of Scotland to mark the creation of the National Cycle Network.

> ❓ *Where did this branch line start and finish? You'll find the answer on information panels along the walk.*

Having passed under the A66, the path then takes to an attractive boardwalk section above the river, before continuing to the site of a former bobbin mill at Low Briery Ⓐ.

The first bobbin mills in the Lake District were opened during the Industrial Revolution in response to the growing demand from cotton and woollen mills of the North. At peak production, Low Briery could produce over 40 million bobbins a year. The bobbins at Low Briery were made from coppiced ash, birch, lime, sycamore and alder. Press on steadily to reach an old railway building on the right (just before a bridge), now used as an information point. Before reaching this, go through a gate on the left, and cross a narrow enclosure to a back lane.

The Vale of Keswick from the summit of Latrigg

Turn left and climb, a little steeply for a while. When the lane/track forks, branch left to a footpath sign (Skiddaw) at a gate and step-stile **B**. Go over a stile beside the gate onto a broad track swinging round gorse bushes, then running centrally up the eastern ridge of Latrigg.

A short way on a plantation is reached, on the right. Just before the end of the plantation, climb left to the centre of the ridge.

A fine promenade now leads across the top of Latrigg to the highest point (which is unmarked, save for a tiny rock outcrop), with stunning views of the Dodds, the central fells, those of the Newlands Valley and the North West, and, to the right, the massive bulk of Skiddaw, Little Man and Lonscale Fell.

From the high point turn northwards and follow a broad grassy track that gradually descends to the parking area at the top of Gale Road **C**. Go through a gate and into the parking area, but soon leave it for a path on the left (The Cumbria Way), that now follows a long, clear and steadily descending course all the way down to a gate at the end of Spooney Green Lane, which soon crosses high above the A66 and runs out to meet a back lane. Turn left and follow the lane, bearing right at a pronounced left bend to return to the railway station parking. ■

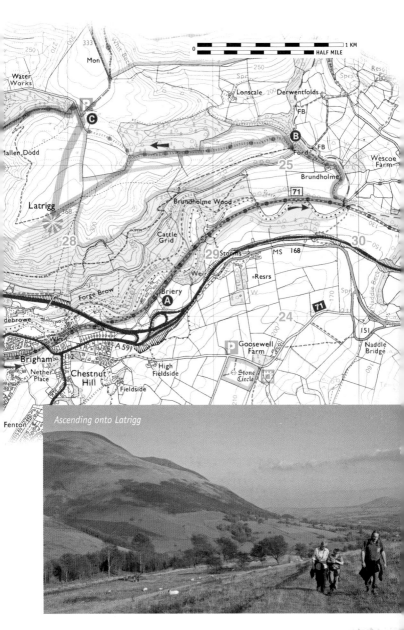

Ascending onto Latrigg

Castle Crag

■ **Cave**
■ **riverside walks**

■ **delightful woodland**
■ **wonderful view**

Commanding a stunning view across Derwent Water to the smooth profile of Skiddaw, Castle Crag is too inviting a prospect to pass by (almost), but its conquest is held in reserve for those who can tackle its steep, slaty path (in both directions). Beyond, woodland wandering awaits, and a riverside amble as good as any in Lakeland.

Castle Crag from beside the River Derwent

walk 20

START Seatoller, Borrowdale

DISTANCE 5 miles (8km)

TIME 3 hours

PARKING National Trust car park at Seatoller (Pay and Display)

ROUTE FEATURES Stony tracks; rocky scrambling (optional); riverside paths; numerous tree roots and rocky sections; one brief, low rocky ledge to cross

GPS WAYPOINTS
- NY 246 138
- Ⓐ NY 242 142
- Ⓑ NY 247 157
- Ⓒ NY 250 165
- Ⓓ NY 252 151

PUBLIC TRANSPORT Bus services daily from Keswick to Seatoller

REFRESHMENTS Seatoller (café)

PUBLIC TOILETS Seatoller car park

PICNIC/PLAY AREA None

ORDNANCE SURVEY MAPS Explorer OL4 (The English Lakes – North Western area)

Leave the car park and turn right to walk up through Seatoller village. Go past the National Park Information Centre at Dalehead Barn, which is well worth a visit, and go out of the village on the Honister road.

At the edge of the village, turn right at a gate giving onto a well-graded track that climbs easily onto the fellside above, heading for a group of four Scots pine, and then swings left to a gate.

Beyond the gate, continue climbing on a stony track, initially beside a wall, until it meets a steeper path ascending from Seatoller below. Go forward onto the middle one of three possible paths (yellow waymark), and ascend close-cropped turf to a gate in a wall corner Ⓐ.

Through the gate turn right onto a path alongside a wall, which gradually leads onward, crossing streams (by footbridges) in the process, to the foot of Tongue Gill, a prominent and deeply cleft valley on the left – once renowned for its quarries. Having gained considerable height, the path affords an airy, invigorating view of Borrowdale and its enclosing fells.

Beyond Tongue Gill, the path, which

remains obvious throughout, heads for Castle Crag directly ahead and framed between distant views of Skiddaw (to the left) and Blencathra (to the right).

B The path starts to descend as it draws level with Castle Crag, and soon a path can be seen rising on the right just before an enormous spill of scree.

? *Who gave Castle Crag to the National Trust?*

Leave the descending track at this point to cross to the path rising steeply, very steeply in places, onto Castle Crag.

Near the top of the climb, the quarry workings that produced all that scree become more evident, and *it is very important to keep younger children under close control here.*

With care, return to the main path below and turn right, heading downhill into the confines of Low Hows Wood. After a gate into the woodland, a narrow footbridge crosses a minor stream that soon joins forces with the River Derwent below. As the river is reached, turn right onto a signposted path for Rosthwaite **C**.

✳ Visitors have been ascending **Castle Crag** for centuries, but none has described the view better than Thomas West in his *Guide to the Lake* published in 1778: 'From the top of Castlecrag in Borrowdale, there is a most astonishing view of the lake and vale of Keswick, spread out to the north in the most picturesque manner ... a beautiful mixture of villages, houses, cots and farms, standing round the skirts of Skiddaw. From the summit of the rock the views are so singularly great and pleasing that they ought never to be omitted.'

Now heading back to Seatoller, the continuing path wanders un-hurriedly through delightful woodland, now close by the river, now

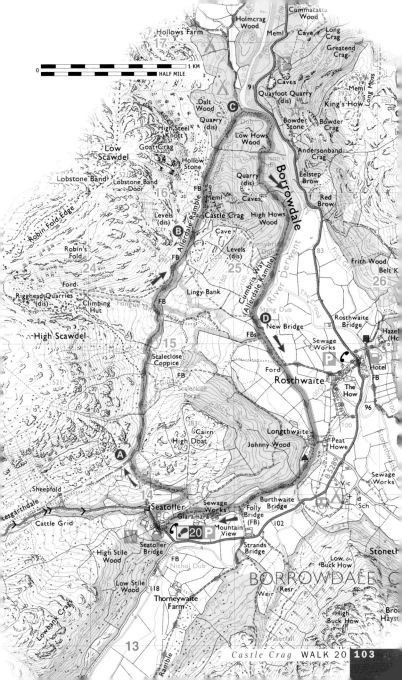

Castle Crag

moving farther away, but never in doubt.

Shortly after turning left at a signpost (still heading for Rosthwaite), an old quarry is encountered on the right, its remains producing an interesting, if rather wet, cave – a tentative peek from a distance is in order, but *closer exploration best avoided, especially by over-inquisitive children.*

Eventually the path breaks free of the woodland, and follows an easy route to a neat single-arch bridge (New Bridge **D**). Do not cross the bridge, but continue riverside, shortly passing a ford. A short section, heavily tree-rooted, preludes the rise of the path onto the top of a flood embankment, where the going is much easier.

Just after a farm, turn right into the grounds of Borrowdale Youth Hostel. Walk in front of the hostel, and onto a riverside path once more. This path seems to lead to an impasse – a rocky shoulder that comes down to meet the river apparently bars progress. Passage is assisted across the first part of this by chains fixed into the rock.

Once across, the path seems to disappear. Not instantly obvious, because a fence appears to block the onward route, the path has actually turned abruptly around the base of a low cliff to a narrow gate.

A good path now leads steadily on and eventually rises to meet a gate through a wall. Turn left and follow a clear path to another gate on the left giving into the car park at Seatoller. ■

Further Information

The hills, mountains and moorlands of Britain, though of modest height compared with those in many other countries, need to be treated with respect. Friendly and inviting in good weather, they can quickly be transformed into wet, misty, windswept and potentially dangerous areas of wilderness in bad weather. Even on an outwardly fine and settled summer day, conditions can rapidly deteriorate. In winter, of course, the weather can be even more erratic and the hours of daylight are much shorter.

Steel End from Braithwaite Lodge, Newlands Valley

Therefore it is always advisable to take both warm and waterproof clothing, sufficient nourishing food, a hot drink, first-aid kit, torch and whistle. Wear suitable footwear such as strong walking boots or shoes that give a good grip over rocky terrain and on slippery slopes.

Tarn Hows

Try to obtain a local weather forecast and bear it in mind before you start. Do not be afraid to abandon your proposed route and return to your starting point in the event of a sudden and unexpected deterioration in the weather. Do not go alone. Allow enough time to finish the walk well before nightfall.

Most of the walks described in this book do not venture into remote wilderness areas and will be safe to do, given due care and respect, at any time of year in all but the most unreasonable weather. Indeed, a crisp, fine winter day often provides perfect walking conditions, with firm ground underfoot and a clarity that is not possible to achieve in the other seasons of the year. A few walks, however, are suitable only for reasonably fit and experienced hill walkers able to use a compass and should definitely not be tackled by anyone else during the winter months or in bad weather, especially high winds and mist. These are indicated in the general description that precedes each of the walks.

Global Positioning System (GPS)

What is GPS?

Global Positioning System, or GPS for short, is a fully-functional navigation system that uses a network of satellites to calculate positions, which are then transmitted to hand-held receivers. By measuring the time it takes a signal to reach the receiver, the distance from the satellite can be estimated. Repeat this with several satellites and the receiver can then triangulate its position, in effect telling the receiver exactly where you are, in any weather, day or night, anywhere on Earth.

Cat Bells reflected in Derwent Water

GPS information, in the form of grid reference data, is increasingly being used in Crimson guidebooks, and many readers find the positional accuracy GPS affords a reassurance, although its greatest benefit comes when you are walking in remote, open countryside or through forests.

GPS has become a vital global utility, indispensable for modern navigation on land, sea and air around the world, as well as an important tool for map-making and land surveying.

Follow the Country Code
- Be safe – plan ahead and follow any signs
- Leave gates and property as you find them
- Protect plants and animals, and take your litter home
- Keep dogs under close control
- Consider other people

(Natural England)

Useful Organisations

Council for National Parks
6-7 Barnard Mews,
London SW11 1QU
Tel. 020 7924 4077
www.cnp.org.uk

Campaign to Protect Rural England
128 Southwark Street,
London SE1 0SW
Tel. 020 798 12800
www.cpre.org.uk

Cumbria Tourism
Ashleigh, Holly Road,
Windermere, Cumbria
LA23 2AQ
Tel. 01539 822 222
www.golakes.co.uk

Cumbria Wildlife Trust
Plumgarths, Crook Road,
Kendal LA8 8LX
Tel. 01539 816300
www.wildlifetrust.org.uk/cumbria

English Heritage
PO Box 569, Swindon
SN2 2YP
Tel. 0870 333 1181
www.english-heritage.org.uk

Forestry Commission
Lakes Forest District, Grizedale,
Hawkshead, Ambleside, Cumbria
LA22 0QJ
Tel. 01229 860373

Friends of the Lake District
Murley Moss, Oxenholme Road,
Kendal, Cumbria LA9 7SS
Tel. 01539 720788
www.fld.org.uk

Lake District National Park Authority
Murley Moss, Oxenholme Road,
Kendal, Cumbria LA9 7RL
Tel. 01539 724555
www.lake-district.gov.uk.

*National Park information centres (*not open all year):*
*Bowness Bay: Glebe Road
01539 442895
Keswick: Moot Hall
01768 772645
*Ullswater: Glenridding
01768 482414

Lake District Visitor Centre
Brockhole, Windermere, Cumbria
LA23 1LJ
Tel. 015394 46601

National Trust (Borrowdale)
The Hollens, Grasmere,
Ambleside, Cumbria
LA22 9QZ
Tel. 01539 435599
Grasmere Information Centre
and Shop,
Tel. 015394 35245

Natural England
Northminster House,
Peterborough PE1 1UA
Tel. 0845 600 3078
www.naturalengland.org.uk

Ordnance Survey
Romsey Road, Maybush,
Southampton SO16 4GU
Tel. 08456 05 05 05
www.ordnancesurvey.co.uk

The Ramblers' Association
2nd Floor, Camelford House,
87–90 Albert Embankment,
London SE1 7TW
Tel. 020 7339 8500
www.ramblers.org.uk

Traveline (bus information):
0871 200 2233

Weathercall
www.weatherline.co.uk

Youth Hostels Association
Trevelyan House, Dimple Road,
Matlock, Derbyshire DE4 3YH.
Tel. 01629 592600
www.yha.org.uk
For Lake District bookings contact:
Tel. 0870 770 6113

Ordnance Survey Maps of the Lake District

Explorer maps: OL4 – The English Lakes – North Western area
OL5 – The English Lakes – North Eastern area
OL6 – The English Lakes – South Western area
OL7 – The English Lakes – South Eastern area

Answers to Questions

Walk 1: A schoolroom

Walk 2: A field guide will help you to identify them, but you should keep an eye open for warblers like chiffchaff, willow warbler and whitethroat, pied flycatchers, redstart and in spring cuckoos, as well as the more commonplace blackbirds and thrushes.

Walk 3: No, it was man-made by damming the outflow of a much smaller lake.

Walk 4: Because it was for the common use of all the villagers, mainly for grazing animals.

Walk 5: Get a leaflet from the visitor centre, and see how many you can identify.

Walk 6: The Brathay.

Walk 8: No height recorded but estimate is about 15 ft (5 m).

Walk 9: Check the view indicator to see how many you got right.

Walk 10: It is from the lake by the dairy pastures, a place where butter was made.

Walk 11: Wordsworth's daughter.

Walk 12: Patterdale.

Walk 13: Bluebell.

Walk 14: Have a look on the information panels and find out.

Walk 15: Have a look at your map and find out. (Maiden Moor and High Spy.)

Walk 16: The Coniston Fells.

Walk 17: Maple.

Walk 18: They are 'dovecotes' to allow doves and pigeons to get in and out.

Walk 19: It ran from Penrith via Keswick to Cockermouth.

Walk 20: Sir William Hamer and his family in memory of his son John.

Crimson Walking Guides

Crimson Short Walks ▸

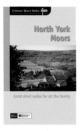
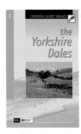
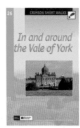
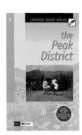

Pathfinder® Guides ▸

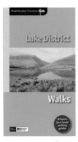
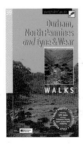
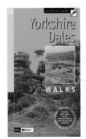

For more information visit www.totalwalking.co.uk
Sales: 020 8334 1730
email: info@portfoliobooks.com